THE BURNING OF
BRINSLEY MACNAMARA

THE BURNING OF
BRINSLEY MACNAMARA

PADRAIC O'FARRELL

THE LILLIPUT PRESS

First published in 1990 by
THE LILLIPUT PRESS LTD
4 Rosemount Terrace, Arbour Hill,
Dublin 7, Ireland

A CIP record for this
book is available from
the British Library

ISBN 0 946640 56 4

Cover design by Jean McCord
Set in 11 on 13 Elegant Garamond by
Tony Moreau, Dublin
Printed by Colour Books Ltd, Dublin

For the people of and from Delvin
– including the Weldons –
and to the memory of Colonel John Kane

For all sad words of tongue or pen,
The saddest are these: 'It might have been!'

John Greenleaf Whittier (1807-92)

CONTENTS

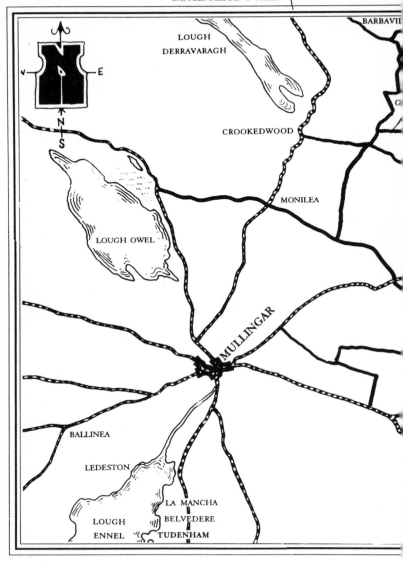

CASTLEPOLLARD 3 MILES

BARBAVII

LOUGH
DERRAVARAGH

CROOKEDWOOD

MONILEA

LOUGH OWEL

MULLINGAR

BALLINEA

LEDESTON

LA MANCHA
BELVEDERE
LOUGH
ENNEL   TUDENHAM

FORE 3 MILES
COLLINSTOWN 1 MILE

○ BOOKER'S LAKE

ELLENSTOWN

CLONYN
CASTLE ● ✕ DELVIN

SOUTH HILL

DYSART ●

KILLULAGH ● ● MARTINSTOWN
ROCKVIEW ●

● BRACKLYN

HISKINSTOWN

RAHARNEY

RATHWIRE ✕ KILLUCAN

MULLINGAR - DELVIN REGION

6 Miles

ILLUSTRATIONS

ACKNOWLEDGMENTS

I wish to thank the people of Delvin and relatives of Brinsley MacNamara for their courtesy and hospitality during my many visits to their homes. I thank also The Minister for Education and her staff, particularly David Gordon, Maura Sheehy and Maura Boggs. Assistance was generously given by Nancy Lenihan, Seamus Leonard, Oliver and Mary Weldon, Benedict Kiely, Mícheál Ó hAodha, Sean McMahon, Seán Mac Réamoinn, Eugene and Carmel Doherty, J.J. Finegan, Desmond Rushe, Catriona Crowe, Olive and Denis Sharkey, Hugh Leonard; Martin Fahy, Manager of the Abbey Theatre, and his assistant Sally Sweeney; Tomás MacAnna, David Nowlan; Stiofán Ó hAnnracháin, Registrar, St Patrick's Training College, Drumcondra; Most Rev. Dr J. McCormack, former Bishop of Meath; Most Rev. Dr M. Smith, Bishop of Meath; Most Rev. Walton N.F. Empey, Bishop of Meath and Kildare; Rev. Joseph Troy, P.P. Delvin; Rev. Ronan Drury, Editor, *The Furrow*; Jonathan Armstrong, Librarian, King's Inns; Eddie Bruton N.T., Seamus Brennan N.T.; staffs of National Archives, National Library of Ireland, State Paper Office, Public Records Office, National Gallery of Ireland, Trinity College Dublin Library, Westmeath Library; Mrs Roper, Lt Col. T. Furlong; Mary, Fergus and Christine Kearney; Larry Poynton, Paddy O'Shaughnessy, Molly Mullen, Brendan Mullen, John Fitzsimons, Willie Bray, Mrs Cruise, Christina Barry, Kathleen Ward, Tony Lennon, *The Irish Times* library; Rev. J. O'Dwyer, P.P. Quin; Rev. Murtagh, P.P. Killucan; Rose Doyle, John Weldon, William Branagan, Patricia Corcoran, Michael McCarthy, Comdt Pat Prendergast, Nigel Cochrane, Lt Col. C. Goggin, *Westmeath Examiner*, *The Irish Times*.

I am especially grateful to Olive Sharkey for her work on the maps and drawings.

Oliver Weldon was most generous in allowing me access to and use of papers and writings. I am also grateful to him and his wife, Mary, for their hospitality. Antony Farrell of The Lilliput Press suggested the book and was always encouraging and enthusiastic. Angela Rohan's editing skills were greatly appreciated.

Apologies to an ever-patient Maureen, for spending most of my 1989 holidays in Delvin and assorted repositories of information, and thanks for her usual meticulous proof-reading. Thanks also to my family for continuing support and to Aisling for assistance with word-processing.

PREFACE

If the book were written (as some day it may be) about the book, and particularly about the reactions that followed the writing of it, then that book would be more interestingly informative than the book itself.[1]

Benedict Kiely here echoes André Gide (1869-1951), who was to demonstrate what he meant in the whorled structure of his 1926 novel *Les Faux-Monnayeurs* (*The Coiners*).

Sustaining the theories of such eminent authors was the daunting challenge facing me when Antony Farrell of The Lilliput Press asked me to write this work about *The Valley of the Squinting Windows*, the early-century, alleged *roman à clef* by Brinsley MacNamara. The accuracy of their predictions became apparent very quickly. On an early visit to Delvin, Co. Westmeath, the supposed Garradrimna of the novel, I spoke to some acquaintances about my mission. They mentioned families who were pro-book and anti-book. One wished to know if I would be informing the parish priest. I came away convinced that, while the community was sensitive about the affair, its study was well worth undertaking.

In a feature on Brinsley MacNamara in *The Irish Booklover*, Séamus Ó Saothraí, a former colleague of MacNamara's, wrote of the great silence pervading Delvin prior to the appearance of the paperback edition of the book:

I finally succeeded in getting some information from a young married schoolmaster in the town of Delvin who, having treated me to a hearty tea, showed me where the post office had been in Brinsley's young days, and where the book had been burned. He told me that the last of the book's 'characters' was still living and had had a couple of heart attacks. This new edition of the book, should she become aware of it, 'would kill her for sure'... The old lady who was supposed to have been one of the book's characters passed away before the year [1964] was out. With her died the last ember in 'the ashes of that bonfire in Delvin', as Peadar O'Donnell called it.[2]

The last ember did not die with her, however, and a gentle probing of the *gríosach* still provokes reactions. For example, throughout my early interviews I was warned constantly about an individual whose response to my research would, I was told, be swift and vicious. Contrary to expectation, I was treated with the utmost civility and courtesy. In a polite, gentle way the hurt endured by the person's family over the years since the book's publication was articulated. That single experience showed me the need for this work; it convinced me that if the facts of the case were made available and unfounded myths debunked, there could be a new approach to *The Valley of the Squinting Windows* and all that it has signified down the decades. I have conducted dozens of interviews, listening carefully and, assessing the degree of consistency in the responses, obtained documentary evidence whenever possible. Requests for anonymity have been understood and respected.

Families whose lives were affected by the book overcame their inclination to remain silent. I thank them for that; just as I thank all who rendered assistance in any way.

Padraic O'Farrell

PROLOGUE

A middle-aged lady stood in a Westmeath cemetery on an autumn day in 1987. The mourners had all but departed. Retired primary schoolteacher, Hannah Fitzsimons, came over to where her pupil of yesteryear was chatting with friends. The subject was Brinsley MacNamara, pen-name of local man John Weldon, and the celebrated writer was being praised. As she had often done during schooltime in the forties, Hannah poked Nancy Lenihan in the back with a clenched fist.

'Why do you want to be talking about that fellow? Didn't he only bring shame to the village?' she chastised. Hannah challenged Nancy to go home, read the book again and telephone her if she found one good person in the story apart from the schoolteacher, presumed to be based on the author's father. Yet in her compendium of local history,[1] Hannah had placed the author first in her list of 'Notable Delvin Personalities' and had displayed no rancour in her appraisal of the man who became notorious for his novel *The Valley of the Squinting Windows*.

During the summer of 1964 a feature-writer for *The Irish Times* arrived in O'Shaughnessy's public house in Delvin. Placing a copy of the infamous book on the counter he asked where he could find someone who knew the background to the controversy. A customer replied: 'Far better to put that book back in your pocket and clear off out of here.' Seamus Leonard, who lives in the school residence once occupied by the Weldons, remembers asking his father about the book and getting 'a clip on the ear'. There are families in and around Delvin who still bear unflattering nicknames, inherited from grandparents allegedly represented in MacNamara's book. Remarkably, continuing silence on the rumpus caused by its publication results in a well-founded theory that some are quite oblivious to the fact.

The Weldon family were affected too. In 1988 a first cousin of the author, John Weldon of Ballinea, was introduced to a Delvin man as 'a cousin of Brinsley MacNamara's'. There was no handshake, just a harsh rebuff: 'If he's anything to that bastard, he's not much good.'

So does *The Valley of the Squinting Windows* warrant the hurt suffered by three generations? During a discussion with Benedict Kiely which formed the Foreword to Anvil Books' (Tralee) 1964 edition, Peadar O'Donnell, recalling the 'bitter experience of an Irish author in the practice of his art', states that, ordinarily, he would be little concerned for an author whose work brought a village out against him; after all, this would offer him a new experience, a new vision of his people. He goes on: 'It is different, however, when as in this case the uproar boils over and hurts an innocent bystander.' Brinsley MacNamara's family were among the 'innocent bystanders' of the time but some might argue that since 1918 thousands of decent people in Delvin have suffered in some way by the scorn brought on them and their town by *The Valley of the Squinting Windows*.

Nellie Weldon, sister of Brinsley MacNamara, bred a Westmeath bull when she commented on the affair: 'It will be remembered forever as long as some people are alive.'

ONE

THE BOY

The shops and houses of Delvin scuttle from the base of a thirteenth-century Norman-Irish castle standing close to a motte which is a century older, the relic of a de Lacy fortress built for Gilbert de Nangle. From the de Nangles sprang the Nugents, one of whom, the 14th Baron Delvin, Sir Christopher Nugent, commanded the forces of the Pale and wrote an 'Irish Primer' for the use of Elizabeth I, while another, Francis, established the Irish province of the Capuchin friars in the seventeenth century.

However well they might have treated those learned men, the people of Delvin were less hospitable towards Brinsley MacNamara when *The Valley of the Squinting Windows* was published in 1918. In the absence of the sophisticated pastimes of a later age, such a rural parish was a natural spawning ground for gossip and malicious speculation and was vulnerable to all the slights, real or imagined, to which a small and easily identifiable community stands exposed.

The Weldons were an Anglo-Irish clan of fourteenth-century settler origin. James Weldon came from Ballinea, three miles west of Mullingar. His father, John (called 'Veldon' locally), married a Connors from Skibbereen, Co. Cork. They farmed and sold produce in Mullingar market. James's nephew still lives near Ballinea.

James started his career as a national schoolteacher in the year 1883 at Killough School, four miles south-east of Delvin. Rev. Joseph Coyne, parish priest of Delvin at the time, made the appointment.

On 18 May 1889 Weldon married a local girl, Fanny Duncan. Originally a Scottish name, the form was sometimes used in Ireland as a synonym of Donegan. Fanny's parents came from Co. Meath to a solid two-storey house on the estate of Howard Fetherston of Bracklyn, a landlord murdered in 1868 on his way from Dublin with writs for sixty evictions. Fr Ledwith, a Delvin curate, officiated at the union with witnesses Essie King and Nicholas and Kate McCormack.[1]

James Weldon was remembered by his daughter Nellie as a gregarious man, fond of good conversation and afraid of thunder. Others recall his being stubborn and proud, inclined to participate in local politics but tipping the forelock to no one. It was thought that a fall from a horse had caused the injury which left him with a limp and needing a cane, seeming also to affect him psychologically. James Weldon's wife, Fanny, was reserved and not inclined to leave the house for a chat with neighbours. She was fond of sewing and fashion, made clothes for her girls and encouraged them to learn needlework and cookery. She taught them to be polite – not to look around while in church or peep through windows when passing houses.

The Weldons lived first at nearby Ballynacor (the Town of the Weir[2]), Hiskinstown, and it was there that their first child, John, was born on 6 September 1890. Five days before that, James was enrolled in St Patrick's Training College, Drumcondra.*

It was not unusual then to undergo training after appointment to a school. James was then in his twenty-eighth year and he got a high rating (First Class, Grade 2 – well above average) at St Patrick's. Later, the family lived at Rockview, Bracklyn, and at Corbetstown (where they paid a rent of £10 per year to a Mr Bobbitt). John was taught by his father and after school on a Friday evening he walked across the fields to the home of his mother's parents.

> There was a gurgling stream by Annasock, and its little shining water would flash a promise of the welcome I always got from my grandmother.[3]

The young boy was skilful at drawing and proudly exhibited cartoons of his father, family and schoolfriends, but it was the satirical sketches of villagers that most amused his grandmother and her *seanchaí* husband. This big Meath man told young John stories about 'Dane' Swift, who had lived a while near Trim, and about the eccentric Adolphus Cooke of Cookesborough down the road towards Mullingar, who believed that his turkeys and dogs were dear departed relatives and that he himself would be reincarnated as a bee.

---

*The registers at the college show enrolment on 1 September 1890. Board of Education documentation gives his period at St Patrick's as 1891-2. He was nominated by the Bishop of Waterford rather than the Bishop of Meath, which suggests some difficulty in obtaining clerical approval.

Of such were the tales of my grandfather. They were my fairy tales, half real, half pure folk imagination. But they left a hunger in my young mind and began to draw it out into the world of larger stories.[4]

Simple pleasures of a country youth included hunting, bird-nesting, watching hawkers and patrons heading for the Mullingar horse-races and, occasionally, marvelling at the circus wagons as they passed by, following the lime trail dribbled from a barrel on an advance cart. When he was eight years old John spent a prolonged summer holiday at Ballinea. It was the centenary of the 1798 Rebellion and he took delight in reading of celebrations in Dublin and pasting pictures of them on his bedroom wall. His 'Veldon' grandmother took a keen interest in his reading and encouraged him to recite from newspapers. His grandfather always asked for the war news and was particularly interested in the Spanish-American War of that year, for he had fought with the Confederates in the American Civil War. John would trot after this solemn man as he tilled the land and complained of its inadequacy compared to the rich soil near Delvin or criticized the difficult landowners in the area, the Robinsons.* Talk of General Robert E. Lee, Gettysburg and New Orleans intrigued the lad and filled him with romantic ideas, while his grandmother's practicality instilled a determination to succeed. Once she chastised him for sketching Wolfe Tone and for his interest in Lord Edward Fitzgerald, dismissing 'the foolishness of history'.[5] Still, the redcoated military that he noticed on fair-days in Mullingar and the gentry riding by in their fine coaches reminded John that conditions had not changed greatly since 1798.

On outings to Lough Ennel, south of Mullingar, he learned the historic tales of King Malachy, said to be buried on Cro-Inis, and took note of the fine houses there – La Mancha, Ledeston, Belmont, Dysart, Bloomfield, Tudenham – all of them owned by Anglo-Irish settlers. Belvedere, the home of Robert Rochfort, Earl of Belvedere (1708-72), was the most interesting of them. Its large Gothic folly, 'The Jealous Wall', had been erected in the mid-eighteenth century to

---

* Captain Hercules Robinson of Rosmead, Castletown Delvin, was High Sheriff of Westmeath in 1843 and owned considerable property in the north of the county. The surname would be given later to an unsavoury solicitor in *The Valley of the Squinting Windows*.

obliterate the view of Tudenham where Robert's younger brother
Arthur lived, whom he suspected of a liaison with his wife.

By that hearthside at Ballinea he heard stories about the Dane,
Turgesius, drowned by Malachy in Lough Owel and about the strange
horse-swimming races held there to celebrate Lughnasa; and of how
Mullingar, the county town, got its name:

> Upon a certain time the steward of Conall, son of Suibhne, came to Luachan
> to demand victuals of him. And Luachan had but one sieve of barley-seed;
> and he said: 'We have not got what you demand of him.' But the steward said
> that they would all be put into the sea of fire unless they found three hundred
> wheaten cakes with their condiment of butter and milk. And Colman said: 'It
> is permitted to thee to be swallowed up by the earth!' And forthwith the earth
> swallowed the steward as he went towards his lord to stir him up against
> Colman ... However, his mother said to Colman: 'My good son, help us, for
> we are in a great plight.' Colman went to the mill with his sack upon him, as
> Colum Cille took the sack upon him to the stone ... Now on his arrival there
> was Conall's corn under the mill and it was wheat. Colman ordered it to cease
> ... but the steward would not do at his bidding. 'Then put it in,' said the cleric,
> 'and we will put [ours] on this side, and God will divide for us.' They did thus,
> and Colman put his hand against the mill and turned it lefthandwise, so that
> thenceforward it has been Mullingar (Wry Mill). And God exchanged the
> corn so that Colman had the wheat and the steward barley. So God's name and
> Colman's were magnified through the miracle.[6]

Other excursions took in Fore, with its Benedictine abbey and 'Seven
Wonders',[7] and Lough Derravaragh, where legend told how the
wicked Aoife changed her stepchildren, Aodh, Fiachra, Conn and
Finola, into swans:

> Here on Derravaragh's lonely wave
> For many a year to be your watery home,
> No power of Lir or druid can now ye save
> From endless wandering on the lonely foam.[8]

When he met a family of Argentinian extraction and listened to
their discourses in a foreign tongue, John Weldon became alerted to
the wide world outside Westmeath. He read avidly and soon absorbed
his father's modest library – all except Sir Walter Scott's Waverley
novels, the very volumes Master Weldon wished his son to read. John
Weldon now began to experience the difficulty of being taught by a
parent and expected to provide an example to the other children. Mis-
behaviour by the 'Master's' or 'Mistress's' child was a heinous crime.

John's mother, too, had reservations about his habit of reading.

> Even if he had indulged in a more full-blooded foolishness she might have excused him, but this was such nonsense as she could make no attempt to understand.[9]

Young John borrowed books where he could, from labourers, domestic servants or stewards of local 'Big Houses': Canon Sheehan, William Carleton, Emmet's *Speeches from the Dock* – there was a certain monotony in the titles available. One source was Tom Tuite of Corbetstown, a returned American to whose daughter the novelist later became godfather. The Killucan Workingmen's Club library in Rathwire Hall operated an unusual system: its members brought along their own books and exchanged them freely, and Weldon availed of this facility. When he was twelve years old John Weldon moved into what he later called the happiest period of his life,[10] and one that sowed the seeds for *The Mirror in the Dusk*[11] and *Return to Ebontheever*.[12]

He absorbed more and more local stories, particularly those of Séimí Growney, a herd, who sat outdoors leaning on a stick and regaling passers-by. His son, James, became a friend of John Weldon's, although eight years older. From Séimí Growney, John Weldon learned about 'The Barbavilla Murder', subject of a House of Commons debate in July 1885 when Charles Stewart Parnell tabled a motion calling for an inquiry into the justice of the trial verdicts in the case.[13]

William Barlow Smythe was an unpopular landowner, with a record for evicting defaulting tenants on his large estate near Collinstown, five miles west of Delvin. He walked to a Palm Sunday service in March 1882 but drove back in the carriage with his sister-in-law and another guest, Lady Harriet Monck. They were within two hundred yards of Barbavilla House when shots were fired, killing Mrs Henry Smythe. A government reward of £2000 failed to elicit information that would lead to an arrest so, desperate to secure a conviction, the RIC fabricated evidence and found men prepared to support it by perjury. During special devotions in Collinstown church held three months after the trial, the wife of one of the perjurers confessed before the Rev. Hugh Behan that she had encouraged her husband to swear falsely.

They liked to think of most shocking things that should be happening in Dublin. They hoped and searched for them industriously every evening. But there was little or nothing ever shocking about local life in the Dublin evening newspapers, nothing that was a patch on the brilliant scandals which, to them, brightened life in other and more daring parts of the world.[14]

In spite of his bookish leanings, John Weldon was lively and outgoing. He 'mitched', robbed orchards, 'lamped' rabbits, poached fish from preserved waters, and played pitch-and-toss using buttons for gambling. When the fit-up shows of Dobells or McFaddens came to Raharney and Killucan, John would steal across the fields to enjoy their drama and excitement. Cricket was a popular game around Delvin, supported by the local gentry, while big home-made bats were used for the less formal 'crickets' played by local youths. John also enjoyed hurling, travelling to matches on a borrowed bicycle. He later fostered its introduction to the parish.

About that time, John became closer to his mother, Fanny. Typical of the refined women of her generation, she dressed in a long black coat over a suit, the skirt of which was flared, dropping to the top of her boots (in summer replaced by shoes with straps). She wore her fine hair in a bun and loved hats. Whenever James Weldon went to Dublin he would take her home an expensive piece of millinery, although he had no idea if it would match anything she had. Her daughter Nellie recalled her mother's 'black suit, stripy blouse and black straw hat which had a watersilk ribbon, a big bow and a pinky bit of a plume standing up on it that matched the blouse'. Regardless of the weather, she carried an umbrella and gloves. As Fanny talked to her son he became aware of her family's strong Gaelic leanings, and she would gently boast, for example, of knowing the Athboy-born scholar, Eugene O'Growney, friend of Douglas Hyde.[15]

Whenever his mother was due to give birth, the local midwife, Brigid Devereaux, moved in. She played games with John, did all the cooking and drank a bottle of stout a day. Mary Ann (Molly) Weldon was born on 30 March 1901 and Brigid was marked on the census form of that year as living with the Weldons. Her vigils provided another source for John's education in the ways of rural life.

*   *   *

The register of Ballinvalley (Male) National School, Delvin, shows that John, James and Patrick Weldon were enrolled there on 2 January 1905. By then their father had been transferred from Killough by Fr Tuite, the parish priest and school manager of Ballinvalley, a man later to feature significantly in the Weldons' lives. John was then in sixth class, James and Patrick in third.

In 1833 the National Board of Education had granted aid of £140 towards replacing the old school, which had been in bad repair. A further £100 was raised locally and the new two-storey building was opened in 1834, with the girls' classroom downstairs and the boys' above accessible by an external flight of stairs.[16] In spite of these improvements, an 1895 inspector's report on the school found that four windows had been broken maliciously and that the schoolroom needed whitewashing, appending the startling observation: 'The seat of the outoffices is completely removed and the place is positively dangerous' (this referred to the lavatory, a convenience consisting of a long wooden seat perched over a concrete trench. The catchment was sprinkled with lime occasionally, and emptied during holiday-time).

Delvin's parish account shows that James Weldon took possession of the Ballinvalley School residence after some overholding by the man he replaced, a Master Duffy. The situation caused bad feeling because Weldon was forced to drive his pony and trap from his home at Corbetstown, five miles distant. £104.19.5 was spent on repairs and an agreement entered upon whereby the new teacher would take possession and pay £5 annually in interest. This was normal practice, the teacher being regarded as caretaker by the manager in order to comply with The Residencies Act of 1875. As in most schools of the time, the principal teacher paid for heating and cleaning and was given a meagre allowance from parish funds towards these expenses.* This led to the practice of schoolchildren bringing a sod of turf each winter day along with their books. Every afternoon during the final class, two boys would leave and bring in a pail of water. One would dip a laurel or yew sprig into the pail and sprinkle the floor, then two or

---

* Weldon's name appears in the Delvin parish account for receipt of sums such as £3.10.0 for heating, seventeen shillings for cleaning and polishing, and eight shillings for repairs to windows, glass, locks and desks.

three others would sweep up the dust, mud or dried cowdung brought in by boots that had crossed fields that morning. Only during the holidays was the schoolroom floor scrubbed thoroughly.

The 'Master' was responsible for organizing all this. Indeed, the principal teacher was often an unpaid servant of the school manager. He officiated at card-drives, took catechism classes after Sunday Mass and drew up the 'Dead List'. Parishioners would pay what was expected; £3 from big farmers, merchants and the like, dwindling to a contribution of one shilling from poor homes. Details of 'parents, brothers, sisters, relatives and friends' would be entered on foolscap purchased by the teacher himself.

James Weldon earned himself the name of being a good teacher, if a hard and sometimes cruel taskmaster. Most of his contemporaries ruled with a tight hand (some say Mrs Barry administered the occasional horsewhipping downstairs in the girls' school), but he lives in Delvin folk memory as one in the habit of striking boys on the ears with his cane. Weldon suffered terribly from his hip defect and the stairs to the boys' school was a trial. 'He should never have been a teacher. Because of his ailment, it was a cruelty to have him teaching children,' said a friend of the family's.[17] Complaints from parents, some anonymous, were received at the school, but allegations of low attendances long before the 'Squinting Windows' incident are not borne out by school records. At that time, however, school attendances generally were low. The Irish Education Act of 1892 had introduced compulsory school attendances but contained many flaws limiting its effectiveness. The Irish National Teachers' Organization reported that up to 50 per cent of children between the ages of six and fourteen were absent from school each day. These were depressed times for the labouring classes in the country at large, with graziers predominating in a declining rural economy. Against such a background, the 'men of no property' of the teaching profession evolved a necessary tradition of severity.

In the controversy that was to develop later, defenders of James Weldon state that a boycott of Ballinvalley Male School took place during the headmastership of his immediate predecessor, Master Duffy, and that there was a history of difficulties between parents and teachers in Delvin, but offer no verifiable evidence to support their argument. School inspectors' reports on Ballinvalley were seldom flattering. There were frequent complaints about the state of 'out-offices'. Duffy was admonished in 1892, 1894 and 1896 for unsatis-factory work; in 1897 he was cautioned for a 'serious offence' – religious instruction was being taught at the wrong time and in the girls' school, leaving nobody in charge of the boys! Indeed, a coachman, John Lyons, who added extra-curricular subjects like Latin and music back in 1849, had the best record of all Ballinvalley's teachers.

*   *   *

The Weldon family made their weekly purchases at the Delvin shops: Tierney, newsagent; Smith, bar and grocery; and Mangan, draper. At Gallaghers, the 'Master' bought tobacco for his pipe. He would sit smoking as he entertained callers, including some Boston relatives who visited occasionally. Accompanied by John's grandfather, they would drive out daily from Mullingar to hear James Weldon's stories and anecdotes. With few exceptions, however, locals seemed to be unimpressed by their teacher-raconteur. The vehemence of their dislike was to manifest itself some years later.

John Weldon remained in sixth class until March 1906 and he spent a further three years in seventh class. This was common in a rural community where work was scarce, and anyone aspiring to a white-collar job stayed on in school until their teachers decided they were fit to face the world. Young James Weldon, for example, went on to complete three years in eighth class and Patrick four years, before being demoted to seventh again for his last year.

> But the straggling, pastoral street of Delvin, and the lush fields that ran up to it from every side to pour out their sleek beasts on fair days, were to know me for another while, and to leave their impression deep and enduring ... It was then that, with some of my new companions, I would gaze, hopeful of some fresh outlet, at the old Courthouse, which some years before had been turned into a Young Men's Hall.[18]

Young John Weldon took a developing interest in the nationalistic fervour that was beginning to sweep the countryside. The Young Men's Hall became a meeting-place and the old de Lacy castle nearby served as a symbolic reminder of domination for the young 'Delvins', as villagers were called. The daring 'cattle-running' exploits of Delvin-born Larry Ginnell (1854-1923) sparked further flame in the young men's blood. Lawrence Ginnell was member of Westminster parliament for North Westmeath from 1906 to 1918. Prior to his sweeping election victory he had organized groups to drive cattle off estates whose landlords refused tenants the right to purchase their holdings at a fair price, and John was taken by his father to witness the return home of the Killulagh cattle-drive prisoners in 1907.

For John, the hall held further significance, and after seeing a travelling company perform *East Lynne*, *The Rebel's Daughter*, *Kathleen Mavourneen* and other melodramas, he joined a group which staged its own plays there. A Sinn Féin friend in Dublin sent him copies of their news-sheet and he read about Longfordman Padraic Colum whose 1905 play called *The Land* had been performed at the Abbey Theatre. Care had to be taken about the type of play the group presented. If its content were controversial the pro-Church committee could bar further use of the hall. A new assistant in Ballinvalley School suggested some historical plays that might be acceptable, and John knew of one, 'a new Robert Emmet play by Henry Connell Mangan [which] had been produced by the National Theatre Society'.[19]

Delvin Dramatic Society won the hearts of their audience with the work, for the story of 'Bold Robert Emmet, the guardian of Erin' was told over dying embers at *céilís*,[20] sung about at fair and market, and graphically illustrated in gaudy colours on mass-produced prints; country folk never tired of recalling the young student's brave rebellion of 1803 when he led a handful of men in an attack on Dublin Castle, the seat of British power. After defeat, arrest, trial and death sentence, he concluded his celebrated speech from the dock: 'When my country takes her place among the nations of the earth, then, and not till then, let my epitaph be written.' John Weldon 'seemed to feel intensely the dignity of the impersonation which was demanded of him. His intonation of the lines seemed to hold a high seriousness ... In the speech of the others there were numerous blunders, and the grandiose language was frequently marred by illiterate pronunciation. But there was a certain eagerness, an amount of enthusiasm which gave the quaint proceeding the atonement of life.'[21] Great, therefore, was the applause for young John Weldon, resplendent in uniform of green jacket, white breeches, high boots with gold tassels, cocked hat, in a posture of arrogant defiance. There were no curtain-calls – just a surge of emotional well-being towards the cast as the audience crowded up onto the stage to shake each member's hand.

To a man, the Delvins admired the performance, but John's father disapproved of his leanings towards the theatre. The patriotism cultivated by the production fuelled a discontent spreading across the country. Jim Larkin's first calls from Dublin in 1907 for an end to social injustice reverberated even in quiet backwaters like Delvin. Cultural nationalists like Douglas Hyde, enthusiasts such as Pearse and D.P. Moran (whose Dublin publication *The Leader* relentlessly promoted the ideal of an Irish-Ireland), and writers like Kerry's Rev. Patrick Dinneen (1860-1934) and Rev. Eugene O'Growney (1863-99), grandmother Duncan's acquaintance, fed the people with the ideals of the Gaelic League. National self-respect and a desire for self-reliance found expression in various forms of opposition to West-Britonism and shoneenism.[22] James Connolly's socialist movement was attracting attention and the Irish Republican Brotherhood (IRB), Arthur Griffith and Sinn Féin commanded growing support.

In 1911 an extraordinary attempt was made to have James Weldon dismissed and some children were taken away to other schools. Eight names appeared on a letter of complaint to the 'Secretaries' of the Board of Education in Dublin. This accused Weldon of giving a man money to buy paraffin oil 'to burn a stack of hay and a hay shifter that belonged to Mr Casey of Hiskinstown', and alleged that he wanted the man to shoot Duffy of Killadoran, his predecessor at Ballinvalley. After taking the 'pledge from drink at a public mission hire [*sic*]', the letter said that Weldon broke it a few months later, was 'drunk in the town every night' and 'had a free fight in a public house and boxed through the yard in the presence of about 20 of his scholars'.[23] Young James Growney initiated legal proceedings on that occasion, it stated, even though he was friendly with John and was a cousin of Mrs Weldon. At least one of the supposed authors of the letter, James Holmes, later wrote to the Board of Education denying having signed or given authority for attaching his name.

The scurrilous allegations were pursued, nonetheless, and Fr Tuite was called upon to submit an explanation. On 9 August 1911 he wrote saying that all the supposed signatories had denied writing the letter. However, he went to considerable pains to describe each individual. Edward Smyth he regarded as a very respectable businessman. Michael Merriman was of 'an adventurous disposition and had a hand in every bit of mischief that happened in Delvin'. Concerning the assault, he stated that Mrs Weldon had had a 'bad miscarriage' some time before and that on the day of the incident, Mr Weldon 'drove into Smyth's yard and there met young Growney who saluted him with "You kicked the belly out of your wife," evidently an allusion to Mrs Weldon's recent illness. Naturally, I would think, Weldon knocked him down on the spot and would have inflicted further punishment had not Mr Smyth intervened.' The parish priest suggested that 'a feeling of delicacy must have prevented Mr W. from giving the plain, unvarnished tale'.

In defence of his schoolteacher, Fr Tuite told how, after the alleged assault, Growney stood in wait for Weldon in a passage, 'armed with a brick and evidently with murderous intent'. The yard-man, however, 'observed his movements and finished his intent'. Growney's legal action, adjourned on James Weldon's application as his summons had not been served in time, was not resumed. The priest reported a rumour that 'Weldon squared Growney by a pecuniary consideration', an accusation denied by the teacher when challenged by him; Weldon claimed that Edward Smyth, to avoid bad publicity for his business, paid Growney the four shillings that the summons had cost him, and persuaded him to drop the case.

Fr Tuite described how the Merrimans had a grudge against Weldon because he had refused to falsify their children's attendance records to qualify them for gratuities paid from parish funds for good attenders. He asked how, short of a sworn inquiry, anything could be proven against James Weldon; and offered the opinion that unless Merriman 'got a conscience since five or six years ago' he would not 'hang anything on his oath'. Tuite cited a case where Merriman had 'organized a conspiracy of perjury to prove an alibi' in a poaching charge and boasted of his having 'burst up the conspiracy'. Fr Tuite's letter made no reference to the charge concerning the shooting of Mr Duffy and when this was pointed out, he replied that because of its absurdity, it had slipped his mind. If the parish priest defended James Weldon, so too did the inspector of police, who also stressed that Growney and Merriman each bore grudges against the teacher and were most likely the sole originators of the letter.

During all this, the Master was placed under further stress by school inspectors' complaints, for which he received reprimands: marking a pupil present when he was absent, neglecting timetables and monthly progress reports, not preparing properly for class. Difficult both at school and in the home, and cantankarous towards those he disliked, James Weldon often drank heavily or lashed out at tormentors with his cane. It is hard to decide whether attitudes towards him in Delvin were the cause or result of his bad temper, but easy to understand a talented son's motivation towards ridicule of such an environment. It was not the letter-writers, however, but others in the parish who were to feel offended by the book. Did the novelist decide to take on a community?

By 1918 John Weldon had left Delvin and was dreaming of writing plays for the Abbey Theatre, 'meeting characters who needed only a very little touch of art to put them upon the stage'.[24]

Hiskinstown, Delvin, MacNamara's birthplace

TWO

THE MAN

When he left Ballinvalley School on 30 June 1909, John Weldon was almost nineteen years of age. The Weldon family then totalled nine. Of the children, John (6 September 1890), James (29 September 1894), Patrick (13 June 1896) and Ellen (Nellie, 5 September 1906) were all born in Delvin parish; Thomas (14 August 1898), Mary Anne (Molly, 30 March 1901) and Fanny (30 September 1903) were born while the family were living at Corbetstown in Killucan parish. Nellie was the only one born while they were in the Ballinvalley residence. She remembered her brothers sharing a room with two double beds, a necessity because the school residence was small – just two rooms upstairs and two below* – little space for an adult mind suffused with romanticism, nationalism and literary ambition. John Weldon enjoyed a final holiday period and then, as winter approached, left for Dublin. His father wanted him to study for the Excise Department of the civil service, at Skerries College, but John's first destination was the Abbey Theatre.

> [He] entered the pit. His eyes were immediately held by the continuous movement of well-dressed people coming into the stalls ... The lights were suddenly switched off, after the orchestra had played the overture, and he was looking at a scene out of the life he knew. He felt a sudden interest. The words of the characters in the play came to him as had the words of his mother and sister in his own home.[1]

The patent for the use of the Abbey Theatre had been granted in 1904 after the formation of the Irish National Theatre Society. At that group's first meeting, on St Brigid's Day, 1 February 1903, W. B. Yeats was elected as its president, with George Russell, Maud Gonne and Douglas Hyde as vice-presidents. The objectives were 'to create an Irish National Theatre, to act and produce plays in Irish or English,

---

*The present occupant, Seamus Leonard, has enlarged the building.

written by Irish writers, or on Irish subjects; and such dramatic works by foreign authors as would tend to educate and interest the public … in the higher aspects of dramatic art'.[2] Almost immediately rifts began to appear, mainly along political lines (later difficulties arose more from artistic differences). In 1904 a wealthy patron, Miss Annie E. F. Horniman, had secured the lease of a small music-hall theatre, The Mechanics' Institute, in Dublin's Lower Abbey Street and an adjacent premises in Marlborough Street. On 27 December 1904 the Abbey Theatre opened there. There was little public interest at first, but by the time John Weldon moved to Dublin in 1909 a tour to England had taken place, full houses had rioted during a performance of J. M. Synge's *The Playboy of the Western World*, productions of works by Molière, Lady Gregory and Lennox Robinson had been staged and 'guineas were offered for standing room in the wings'[3] during performances of George Bernard Shaw's *The Shewing-Up of Blanco Posnet* in August 1909. This work had been condemned by the Lord Chamberlain on grounds of blasphemy but its adroit author realized that the Whitehall writ on censorship did not run in Dublin.

As John had suspected, his tutorials for the 'Excise' proved less attractive than the National Theatre. Nor was he happy with his lodgings; they were uncomfortable and his fellow lodgers were unfriendly and inclined to sneer at his country ways. So he discovered the National Library in Kildare Street:

> it was very pleasant to go there and to feel himself being gradually carried away by the dream that came out of all the books. He read every book that took his fancy… He was a well known figure coming into the reading room [and was] fond of sitting down by the side of … Thomas MacDonagh … Padraic Colum… Sheehy Skeffington and Padraic Pearse.[4]

John Weldon's neglect of his studies became sadly apparent, so he auditioned for the Abbey Theatre. The description of this encounter in *In Clay and in Bronze* thinly disguises his interviewer, Lennox Robinson. John was considered good material for the Abbey type of pastoral play, and on 22 September 1910 he was cast as a rebel in a revival of *The Piper*. In the Norreys Connell one-act, young Weldon shared the stage with Fred O'Donovan, Marie O'Neill and the great Arthur Sinclair. The main offering of the evening was Synge's *The Well of the Saints*.

Within a week, John Weldon, now appearing under the stage-name of Brinsley MacNamara,* played his first lead role at the Abbey: Denis Barton in R. J. Ray's *The Casting Out of Martin Whelan*, which was staged on 29 and 30 September and 1 October. The eccentric Dublin theatre first-nighter and diarist Joseph Holloway approved, stating:

> An actor new to the Abbey Company – Brinsley MacNamara – was excellent as 'Denis Barton' and got a round of applause on his exit in Act 1 and a call at the end of the act.[5]

Brinsley MacNamara's first venture into the classics was in Lady Gregory's translation of Molière's *L'Avare* (*The Miser*), where he played the broker, Master Simon. Then followed minor roles in Lady Gregory's *The Rising of the Moon* and Synge's *Riders to the Sea* (in which he shared the stage with Sara Allgood who played Maurya). Revivals of the Shaw and the Lady Gregory kept him in work till the end of the year. He visited Delvin occasionally and did not endear himself to some villagers as he strolled down its only street dressed in broad-brimmed hat and red-lined cloak. Already, village wags were taunting drinking companions, saying Brinsley was 'doing a right take-off' of them on the city stage.

The second decade of the new century opened with Brinsley playing a porter in another Lady Gregory Molière translation, *The Rogueries of Scapin* (*Les Fourberies de Scapin*). After a succession of minor parts, he must have relished his role as the blind piper in Padraic Colum's *Thomas Muskerry* during March. In July his poem 'The Silent Change' appeared in the *Sunday Independent* – at the time of his father's ordeal at home (described in the previous chapter). Brinsley appeared in no more National Theatre productions until the American tour which began on 27 January 1912 in Indiana and continued through Illinois, Chicago and Boston until 4 March. While Arthur Sinclair and Sara Allgood played the blind couple in Synge's *The Well of the Saints*, Brinsley was in a minor role of villager. A juryman in *The Shewing-Up of Blanco Posnet*, he was promoted to foreman during the play's run at Plymouth (Mass.), landing-place of the Pilgrim Fathers.

---

* Chosen on an impulse, it incorporates Richard Brinsley Sheridan, whose play he was attending, and a relative of his mother's whom he had just met.

Brinsley was back on the Abbey stage in Dublin during March, although the remainder of the company did not return from the United States until May. Joseph Holloway later wrote:

> Arthur Sinclair came over ... and had tea with us. He spoke of Brinsley MacNamara and his playing the role of self-appointed advance agent to the Abbey in the States in order to touch people, until he became such a nuisance that the company made up his fare and something over and sent him back to Ireland. Now he is turning and reading them in the press for their kindness. He may have talent but he is very lazy. He was on the Boston Transcript for a while. On the first tour he was engaged as understudy, but when he was called upon to play Morgan's part in *The Image* it was found he hadn't learned it at all.[6]

This diatribe was penned on 2 May 1913 and may have been coloured by MacNamara's failure to support a proposal to publish Holloway's diaries. During the tour, indeed, Lady Gregory made use of MacNamara for secretarial work, typing scripts etc. His acting career ended in April 1912, but during that summer he wrote his account of the American tour for the *Irish Independent*.[7] Two poems followed, 'Old Connor' and 'The Crude Rhyme of the Tinker's Wife'.[8]

> He was not sorry to leave behind that jumbling together of great facts which was represented by America. But the roar of it was still in his ears and the dazzling show of it was still in his eyes. [And back in Dublin] there were the poets, critics, artists, scholars, journalists, professors, and all the miscellaneous hangers-on of literature who might be inclusively termed 'The Dublin Decadence' still in the various stages of repose in which he had left them.[9]

Soon, however, he decided that the life-style of Dublin's literati was not conducive to productivity. Lodgings, whether in South Circular Road, Mountjoy Square or the Iveagh Buildings, were spartan and he was short of money and food. He wearied of the long hours of drinking and literary disputation, paying court to whoever was in fashion – each day 'sitting in exactly the same positions at the tables, taking their usual quantity of drink and contributing their customary remarks to the symposium'.[10] Dublin was full of intolerant upper classes, he decided, although he was then attending to one of its celebrated daughters, the artist Grace Plunkett. Even if it seemed like defeat, he would have to return to Delvin.

He wrote telling his mother of his intention, relations with his father being strained to the point of silence since his decision to abandon an Excise career for the stage. Nellie Weldon, who was playing in the yard when her brother walked down the short boreen to the family home, found it difficult to recognize the tall man in the coffee-coloured suit, cream shirt, yellow tie and tan shoes. Last time she had seen him he had hidden a rag doll in the family cradle; this time his gift was a bag of sweets. She ran to fetch her mother, who was pumping water for the cattle. Aware of the tension his return home might cause, Mrs Weldon displayed no excitement.

> He had expected a warmer welcome, and now some of the inevitable constraint he had dreaded all the way from Dublin was upon him.[11]

If his mother was astonished by John's 'swankee' suit then, she soon had to accustom herself to his new style of dressing and long silences as he dwelt on some piece of writing or other. But his sense of humour is apparent from a letter written to the poet Seamus O'Sullivan on 18 July 1914:

> Yes, I have recently moved into an east room and find myself greatly improved by the change. Here in the village, I have made a study of this matter of light and have already cured one man of sleeplessness and another of neuropenia, by making them change their rooms and find that the most successful people are those with a west light. Among those who are with a north or north-east light are bankrupts, drunkards, lunatics, defectives and decayed people.[12]

Over the next four years he wrote prolifically and had articles and poems published in various national newspapers and magazines. In spite of this output, however, he seemed to miss city life. His nostalgia is thinly disguised in a letter to Joseph Holloway (dated 23 September 1917) in which he explains how late harvesting operations owing to heavy rain prevented his coming to Dublin:

> since my retirement to the life of the fields, these are the things that most intimately concern me. I have not been in Dublin since I last saw you there ... In this place, as you can imagine, I am altogether isolated from the literary and the journalistic world. I never see any paper but the *Independent* and even that, only occasionally. Until my return to Dublin, I wish to preserve my isolation from all things, so, should you be speaking to any of my former friends from the Abbey, I trust you will not mention anything of my present whereabouts ...
>
> Very sincerely yours,
> Brinsley MacNamara[13]

His father, whom Brinsley was convinced had never read any of his articles or poems, was then receiving 'Efficient' ratings (with 'No Irish taught' tagged on) from inspectors. He still wished his son would find more reliable employment, even suggesting that Brinsley might use the influence of his friend Tom Kettle to obtain a commission in the British army.* Brinsley answered no trumpet-call to war but had embarked upon a project that would bring conflict on to the street of Delvin. For three months, June, July and August 1916, he worked feverishly on a novel, the plot of which had been forming in his mind for some time. Less than two years later *The Valley of the Squinting Windows* would stir his native village into violent action. Nellie Weldon recalls:

> He used to write that book in the school in the evenings; he'd bring over the keys and be over the remains of a fire. All the writings were in the small leather bag he brought from America, and that was locked and was under his bed and he only brought it over to the school; he never brought it out at night. He'd go for a walk afterwards; sometimes he might play cards.
>
> I used to bring over his tea to the school, and the basket would be hitting the ground – a big basket, he was very fond of tea. There would be a fry and everything, with a pot of tea, a bottle of milk; the whole shoot would be in the basket. I'd be leaving it down every minute. I remember one evening there was thunder and lightning. There was a big flash of lightning; I didn't mind that but when the clap of thunder came, I nearly dropped the basket. My mother would say 'Don't let anybody see you going up the stairs'; you see, there was a big stairs outside at the front – on the left-hand side from the road, and there was a railing, the boys used to slide down [it]. But there'd hardly be anybody passing at that time of evening. I used to tip at the door [and leave him the meal].[14]

Tom Lenihan, small farmer and auxiliary postman, lived at Ellenstown, half a mile north of Delvin. He was married to Mary Byrne of Moyleroe, for whom John Weldon once had 'a rag on the bush'. Weldon never expressed his affection, however, and lost out to his more vigorous friend. They remained close, and some suggest that most of the book was written in Lenihan's kitchen, a mistaken belief that may have arisen because of John Weldon's frequent visits.

---

* Brinsley had met this barrister, professor of national economics at UCD, member of parliament for East Tyrone, fervent nationalist and Volunteer (he was killed fighting at the Somme in September 1916), during his earlier visits to the National Library.

With the excitement of coming to the end of his novel, Brinsley worked into the night. A refugee in the schoolhouse, he used a carbide lamp, keeping it well shaded, for his father still complained about his wasting time around Delvin when he should be chasing a civil service job.[15]

Mystery surrounds the immediate source of Brinsley MacNamara's inspiration, and is deepened by a letter to George Roberts, managing director of Maunsel's, in September 1917. Edward MacLysaght had read the manuscript and recommended its acceptance but Roberts was wary of possible libel in the opening chapter. (It was Roberts who five years earlier had rejected Joyce's *Dubliners*, and destroyed the printed sheets at Maunsel's before its eventual publication by Grant Richards in June 1914.) Brinsley's letter read:

Ballinvalley
Delvin
Co. Westmeath
Sept 23rd 1917

Dear Mr Roberts,
The point raised in your letter, and note on passage in Chapter One of 'The Squinting Windows' is very interesting. However, here are the facts upon which this portion of the story is based.

Mr Henry Shannon and Mr Robinson, the solicitor, were as they actually existed here in Westmeath about thirty years ago – bosom companions and first cousins. Mr Robinson afterwards became Crown Solicitor for the county. When Henry Shannon got himself into the scrape with the girl, he went to his legal friend for advice. Whatever that advice may have been, the taking of her to Dublin was what he did as a result of it, as the people of the locality understood it. This amounted to 'making a prostitute of her' and it was in this light that she afterwards came to see herself, because of the scorn of those around her and because of Mr Robinson's letter. Mr Robinson's advice was merely that of a shrewd man with a perfect knowledge of the people of the Valley, and his letter the best means of frightening her from further action in the circumstances he had helped to create.

In the bit I have now in, I think I have fully indicated the essential portion of these facts and removed from this portion of the story any trace of legal error which may have existed. This alteration will not necessitate corresponding alterations in other parts of the story. I trust you will find it satisfactory.

Sincerely yours,
Brinsley MacNamara[16]

It has been argued that this was a plausible concoction designed to set a circumspect publisher's mind at rest, but given its specificity it is worth following some of the leads offered. Possible models for the crown solicitor were John Julian (1860-92), Robert H. Todd (1894-1903), P. R. Kelly (1904-15) and Thomas J. Dowdall, incumbent when the book was being written. Brinsley's siting of the incident thirty years previously would rule out Julian, for he was already crown solicitor in 1887, while Kelly and Dowdall would have been too young at the time. Todd, who resigned from office on 10 January 1903, issued a summons in a case involving a Rev. Dardis, accused of rape. Folk reports around Delvin centre on a child born out of wedlock and the burial of an infant in a shoebox or in Booker's Lake; a charge of infanticide is mentioned but not supported. So if there was issue as a result of the rape, Todd's name might have been tied in with the speculation. Other versions of a possible source point to a child being born to a clergyman's housekeeper. These are confused and are not helped by some remarkable coincidences.

For example, a Rev. John Robinson (the surname given to the solicitor in the novel) came to Delvin as RC curate in 1899 and served only a year before leaving for Australia and America. His name is linked with another departure to Australia, that of a pregnant, single girl named Fitzsimons.

A second Robinson, Captain Hercules of the Clonyn estate, near Ballinvalley, was warden at St Mary's Workhouse in 1839 and 1847. It is said that he was also joint manager of Ballinvalley School and that the parish priest, Fr Fitzgerald (also the name of the contemporary Protestant rector), had him charged with committing adultery with his housekeeper. The local press and an *Irish Times* report on the subsequent trial states that an incident of eighty years earlier was at the core of *The Valley of the Squinting Windows*, which would reinforce the Hercules Robinson theory.

A Roman Catholic parish priest of Delvin, Rev. James Savage (who too shared a surname with the rector of the time), was suspended in 1858. One opinion is that he had got a girl pregnant while others, pointing out that village folk always felt strongly about clergy, contend he was maligned. He cursed his parishioners before leaving them and said that only those who supported him would prosper. Local sources give examples of wealthy families whose forefathers spoke in favour of the priest.

With such a confusion of names and incidents, and in the absence of documentation relating to the suspension and transfer of clerics, the origin of the incident at the core of *The Valley of the Squinting Windows*, if it is factually based, remains obscure. Brinsley's revisions proved acceptable and the novel went into production.

Ireland's historical watershed, the 1916 Easter Week Rising, had taken place while the novel was being written. The country was undergoing a conscription crisis and heading towards its War of Independence as final proofs were arriving in Delvin. Still wary of his father, Brinsley would meet the postman outside the school residence. He kept more and more to himself, and the neighbours would peep through the hedge at the 'Master's bearded son wandering around the garden reading – mixing with a crowd in Dublin who were putting on plays as far away as Boston. Wandering and reading, sure signs of dementia.'[17]

Beyond Westmeath and Ireland, the Great War in Europe was reaching its bloody climax. In March 1918 the German offensive against the British opened on the Somme; a second thrust came on 8 April and lasted until the 25th. The *Vindictive* was sunk and the final German offensive against the French had been launched. A quieter launching, without celebration or publicity, took place in Dublin in May. Without their knowing it, Maunsel and Company released a bombshell, and Delvin would never be the same again.

Clonyn Castle, Delvin, site of the reading

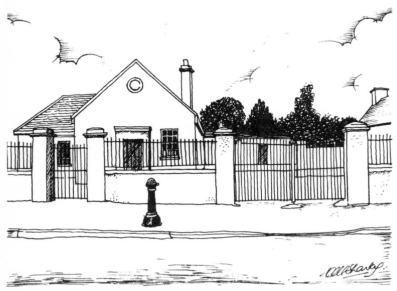

Market House yard, Delvin, site of the burning

THREE

THE BURNING

Accounts of what occurred on the evening of 28 May 1918 are as varied as they are interesting. Hannah Fitzsimons[1] and Nellie Weldon[2] both state that it began with a group of ladies sitting in the sun on the steps of Clonyn Castle outside the village, reading the new book by Jack Weldon. Delvin had lauded his effort. He was a local boy made good and the idea of having a real author in their midst was appealing. Few copies of the book had reached the locality and this was one of its earliest public readings. Fitzsimons suggests that they were all members of well-to-do local families. Others insist the females were members of the domestic staff and would not be fluent readers. In any event both reader and listeners readily supplied models for MacNamara's village gossips, seven sleek publicans, gombeen men, flirtatious shop-boys, spoiled priest and assorted characters:

> Bursts of laughter punctuated the reading as one or other called out, 'That's N. to a tee' or 'There's no mistaking who that is!' But suddenly the reading stopped at p. 48. There was no mistaking to whom this referred! The listeners now looked at the stony face of the reader. The book was closed with a bang; the shocked ladies stood up and almost wordlessly made their way home.[3]

The offending page had described Garradrimna's postmistress steaming open and resealing a letter:

> Then the temptation that was a part of her life would prove too strong for her and a look of longing would come into the dull eyes as she went hobbling into the kitchen to place it over the boiling kettle and so embark it upon its steamy voyage to discovery. In a few minutes she would be reading it, her hands trembling as she chuckled in her obscene glee at all the noble sentiments it might contain.
>
> The subsequent return of the letter to the envelope after the addition of some gum from a penny bottle if the old sticking did not suffice. Her interludiary sigh of satisfaction when she remembered that one could re-stick so many opened envelopes with a penny bottle of gum by using it economically.[4]

Another version records Joseph Clyne, publican and butcher, regaling his bar-room customers with episodes from the new book, and the bawdy jeers and whoops of hilarity as villagers are recognized in its pages. If the similarities were not immediately apparent, Clyne pointed them out. Midway through the sixth chapter he too stammered to a halt, again on page forty-eight:

> It was thus and thus that Rebecca Kerr ran through her mind a few immediate sketchy realizations of this village in Ireland. She had lived in others, and this one could not be so very different ... There now was the butcher's stall, kept filthily, where she might buy her bit of beef or mutton occasionally. She caught a glimpse of the victualler standing with his dirty wife amid the strong-smelling meat. The name above the door was that of the publichouse immediately beside it.[5]

If Joseph Clyne had read on, he would have come across as harsh an indictment as could be aimed at any country couple. Describing 'the publican and victualler's wife' MacNamara had written:

> She was the hardest woman in Garradrimna. Her childlessness had made her so. She was beginning to grow stale and withered, and anything in the nature of love and marriage, with their possible results, was to her a constant source of affliction and annoyance ... She took the letter from her flat bosom, where she had hastily thrust it, and looked at it from every possible angle. It seemed to possess a compelling attraction. But she could not open it here. She would run across to her friend the postmistress, who had every appliance for an operation of the kind ... Soon the bespectacled maid and the barren woman were deep in examination of Rebecca Kerr's letter to Ulick Shannon.[6]

Mrs Clyne, it was said, had lost two children at birth and indeed the couple were still childless after many years of marriage.[7]

Clyne's fury at being ridiculed was fanned by being the instrument of his own exposure. He reacted by offering drinks to all present and then urging them into action. The removal of the remains of a young man from Killough, Vincent Hegarty, had drawn a crowd to Delvin and to Clyne's that May evening.

Despite the appeal of these dramatic accounts of spontaneous indignation, an uncredited feature in the *Westmeath Independent* of 8 August 1964 states:

> In rural Ireland there is an old sporting maxim that once a hare is raised it will either be chased to the kill or beaten into the escape. And so it was in the case of *The Valley of the Squinting Windows*. Anonymous letters were received by

the editors of the various newspapers and magazines to which [MacNamara] regularly contributed. Natives of the village who were resident in other parts of the country and those who were in exile were asked to add their voices to the protest against the book and the man who wrote it. Preliminary steps were taken to bring an action for libel and when these were discontinued more immediate methods were employed.

The *Independent* article and certain evidence in court later suggest a period of plotting before any overt aggression, and this is likely, given that copies of the book did reach the area. The writer described 'a general feeling of frightfulness steadily [mounting] to breaking point on the evening of May 28'. Brinsley MacNamara had told him: 'If I had been found that evening I would have been murdered. They were mostly all wild with liquor and carried various implements of destruction, including revolvers which were freely discharged.' An RIC sergeant claimed at the trial that he had had a patrol in readiness, reinforcing the theory that trouble was expected.

The mob, consisting of at least one member from almost every house in Delvin, gathered (either from the funeral, at the behest of the lady readers or having been disgorged from Clyne's public house) and menacingly approached James Weldon, who was on the footpath chatting to Thomas North, the saddlemaker. Weldon, it appears, was suspected of having a hand in the writing of the novel, some even regarding him as the sole author. According to one account the teacher took on his aggressors and put up a stout defence. Others state that North, sensing trouble, brought James Weldon indoors and that, seeing this, the mob guessed correctly that his son was within. In any event, the author escaped quickly, hid awhile in Tierney's stable, then sped by a circuitous route towards Martinstown Hall, a mile and a half away, where the Delvin branch of the Irish Volunteers was accustomed to meet. (The ardent nationalism evident during Delvin Dramatic Society's grand presentation of the Robert Emmet/Sarah Curran epic had abated in the wake of the 1916 Rising. Drilling and meetings still took place but Volunteers were being arrested on foot of alleged treasonable communication with Germany in the infamous 'German Plot'.)

Part of the Delvin mob, realizing what was happening, went to the hall to flush out the author. Forewarned again, MacNamara had left for his uncle's place in Ballinea – a journey of fourteen miles across country. Some say there was a fight with the Volunteers who supported Weldon; but most agree that the crowd contented itself with calling on the Volunteers to picket Ballinvalley School the next morning in order to eject James Weldon. Opinion was split amongst the Clubmen and, having failed to obtain any assurance, the Delvin deputation withdrew.[8] As motorcycles scoured the countryside all night for Brinsley MacNamara, back in the village the situation deteriorated.

> When the crowd came up, two of the defendants, Corcoran and Clyne, who were the leaders of that particular mob, began to shout, 'Let us drive him out' and the crowd shouted 'Drive him out!' Halpin and Clyne seized [James Weldon] and were about to pull him out of the shop and beat him when the police interfered, and [Weldon] was able to escape by the back door ... The crowd then headed by Halpin and Clyne, and containing most, if not all, of the defendants, went to Father Tuite at the Parochial House, and saw him there. They then came back to the Market Square and held an indignation meeting there.[9]

To make matters worse, Fr Tuite, parish priest and school manager, was not very supportive of their call for action. This country clergyman of the old order had already taken his place in diocesan folklore when he moved to Delvin from Coole, which was then called by the name it bore in the *Tripartite Life of St Patrick* – Mayne. After Fr Tuite's first offering day* in Delvin, he was disappointed with his new flock's lack of generosity. He alluded to it at Mass the following Sunday: 'The only comment I will make is that you are worse than Mayne.'[10] The 76-year-old priest had served as a curate in the parish from 1884 to 1889, and as parish priest from 1892, so he knew the temperament of the people confronting him. He was on good terms with the teacher (it was he who had transferred him from Killough to the better appointment at Ballinvalley), but the crowd at his hall door were 'impassioned to get rid of Weldon'.[11] The priest pointed out that it was not easy to dismiss a teacher who had performed his duties adequately. According to Tom Lenihan's evidence at the subsequent court hearing, Clyne asked: 'Fr Tuite, are you going to allow Master Weldon to teach school in Ballinvalley?' Patrick Corcoran challenged further: 'If you do, Fr Tuite, we won't.' Lenihan's concluding words evoke an older and better-chronicled trial by mob rule. He claims that Fr Tuite capitulated,

---

*In which a church collection is made to supplement the living of the attendant priest.

saying, 'Very well, do as you like.'[12] A village's Pilate had washed his hands, only temporarily, but for long enough to pass control to the angry ringleaders, who began planning further action. Tom Lenihan, for example, was given a choice between removing his children from the school and taking his cows from Patrick Corcoran's field.

Older people in Delvin today remember hearing that James Weldon returned to Ballinvalley while the mob conferred with the priest. None has any recollection of shots, despite Brinsley MacNamara's report of 'revolvers which were freely discharged'. There is adequate evidence, however, of the classic expression of displeasure reserved for unpopular literature:

> a pall of smoke hung over the village [and] in the Market Square a shouting crowd encircled a blazing tar barrel. Despite the tumult, the occasion possessed an element of ceremony. Loud voices were hushed momentarily as an object was thrown into the leaping flames. Then came the inevitable cheer. The village had made its protest.[13]

The children playing their hopscotch or ghost-in-the-garden on the street that evening wondered what all the commotion was about. In later years they were told of the book-burning and of the ritual observed: an order was decided in accordance with the degree of grievance. Thus it is said that the 'hardest woman', made so by her childlessness, the 'filthy butcher's' wife, Anne Clyne, was accorded the honour of burning the first copy.* Such a public admission of identification and offence is unusual among rural folk; an ashamed reticence or blank denial of association would be far more normal.

> The great night of the final chapter had almost come. The whole book had been transferred, bit by bit, from the school to the cottage. He had brought home the two last chapters the night before, but she had been so affected by the second last that she rushed off to bed early ... She hurried into the room where the last chapter was waiting to be read. It didn't take her long ... When she had got down to the copperplate flourishes, which she felt must mean the word 'Finis' and the end, she knew there was only one thing to be done. She locked the door and began to put on a huge heap of a fire. When she had it blazing she brought the pile of manuscript out of the room and tore it in temper, page by page. She enjoyed seeing the words ... fading quickly out of existence in the flames. When it was all just one black, shivery mass she felt she could face Castletown again.[14]

---

*Another claim was made later. See p. 107.

Newspaper coverage of the controversy was tardy and muted. The national press payed it little attention, while the local *Westmeath Examiner* did not carry a report until 22 June. Its headline read:

THAT 'VALLEY'

-and-

Those 'Squinting Windows'

–

Publication of a New Book

–

And its Remarkable Sequel

–

The piece adopted a cautious approach, announcing:

> Delvin has for some time past been in the limelight in a rather unusual manner. A great deal of excitement and, at times, local scenes have taken place [*sic*], and reliable information further indicates that many prominent local people have felt aggrieved.
>
> Now, the whole truth has, it seems, had its origin in the publication of a certain book – to wit, a recently issued volume entitled, 'The Valley of the Squinting Windows'. It is from the pen of one 'Mr Brinsley McNamara' [*sic*], and is not the first work from that rather facile writer. 'Brinsley McNamara' is, however, only a *nom-de-plume*, the author's real name being Weldon, he, in fact, being a son of the Ballinvalley National (Male) School Teacher, Mr James Weldon.

This judgment of the author's work as 'facile' may well have been coloured by an uncomplimentary reference in the novel to the local newspaper:

> He strolled up the street towards the old castle of the de Lacys. The local paper, published at Mullaghowen, was never tired of setting down its fame. The uncouth historians of the village had almost exhausted their adjectives in relating the exploits of this marauding baron of the Normans …[15]

The local reporter continued:

> This fact and the knowledge that 'Brinsley McNamara' has resided a good while in Delvin, in conjunction with observations on the nature and descriptions contained in the book in question, have, it appears, convinced popular feeling in Delvin that the venue of its 'Valley of the Squinting Windows' is none other than the historic old village of Castletown Delvin,

and its surroundings, and the personages and characteristics described are intended to satirise or point to residents in that place or its vicinity.

—

As to the value of these conclusions drawn by the public of Delvin, or what grounds the work supplies for such deductions, no word of comment or opinion of any sort is here tendered. These notes are merely concerned with the facts that the book having been published, Delvin public opinion seems to have shaped itself as above in regard to it and that an undoubted feeling of hostility (on which no criticism whatever is offered) towards the writer of the book and his father, arose as a result leading to certain incidents ...

The book aforesaid, having been issued a few months ago, was reviewed in several daily and other newspapers, and criticism on the work, on its literary merits, of course, and without any idea of whether the author had any particular place or people in his mind's eye, was, for the most part, favourable.

These paragraphs show the evasiveness of contemporary reportage, but an antagonism towards the author and his father can be discerned as the story develops:

An interesting report has also come to hand in regard to the whole matter. It is that a number of the local folk in Delvin, including some of those who believe they have a grievance against the author of the book 'The Valley of the Squinting Windows,' have foregathered in solemn conclave on more than one recent occasion and discussed the situation. Their grievance against the work is that it indicates localities and persons in Delvin and district, and conveys charges of a serious character against these persons, who deny and repudiate the allegations made in the book, as, indeed, in reference to the habits and characteristics of imaginary personages – but which the aggrieved Delvin folk maintain are aimed at one and another of their number, professional, commercial, labour etc.

—

It is understood the private meetings in question decided to take active steps, and that a copy of the book has already been submitted to counsel with the object of ascertaining if legal proceedings against the publishers or the author, or both, should be embarked upon.

The *Midland Reporter* and *Westmeath Nationalist* of the time was reporting the German Plot and latest news of the Great War. Its edition of 6 June described a presentation made by Volunteers and Cumann na mBan members at Martinstown Hall to Robert Nugent of the Delvin Corps of the Irish Volunteers and member of Delvin Defence Committee. Lawrence Ginnell was among the speech-makers. Not until 20 June did it mention the burning, then merely running a piece that had appeared in *The Irish Times* two days previously:

> Politics do not occupy the whole attention of disturbed Ireland. There is trouble upon the Midlands, particularly upon Westmeath, and it has nothing to do whatever with raids for arms and cattle-driving,[16] with Lord French's proclamation or with Conscription. It is all about a book, 'The Valley of the Squinting Windows', recently published in Dublin, the author of which, Mr Brinsley MacNamara, is a native of Delvin in Westmeath. Mr MacNamara is accused of having drawn from life in Delvin for his novel – a highly 'realistic' work the people of which, as a reviewer in the *Irish Times* has pointed out, show no redeeming virtues.[17] Copies of the book reached Delvin and presently what is called the 'Rebellion of the Squinting Windows' broke out. The brunt of the attack fell upon the author's father, a schoolmaster. The 'rebels' marched down to the school and attempted to evict Mr MacNamara [*sic*] senior.
>
> In this they were not successful … The population of the place is by no means united in approving these drastic measures of literary censorship and the event has led to the breaking up of the Sinn Féin and Volunteer Organizations the leaders of which discouraged the 'rebellion'. The book itself, unpleasant though it is, does not touch at all upon political questions. What seems to be objected to is, partly, the satire on gombeenism and partly the fact that the central incident of the story, or something like it, actually happened in Delvin about eighty years ago.

Obviously the newspaper reports on the events of 28 May 1918 would not have attracted attention towards the controversy from outside Westmeath. National and international news was capturing the headlines and a village quarrel was of little significance. The notoriety which *The Valley of the Squinting Windows* still enjoys emerged from far more serious events.

'Would your mother have preferred if he had never written the book?' radio interviewer John Skehan asked Nellie Weldon in 1988. 'I think she would,' replied Nellie. 'She was very fond of him. He was very kind and good-natured and very good to his parents.' At eighty-two years of age, shortly before her death on 8 August of that year, Nellie recalled the evening of the burning:

> They took Father out of North's and beat him up. [John] was in the hall and got word. He left and went to grandfather on the other side of Mullingar – Ballinea. They were going to attack him. Father got his glasses broken. They were all drunk; all plastered. Toughs! Father had nothing to do with the book. He didn't even know [John] was writing it.

She drew a comparison with the 'crowd who went to the Tralee Tribunal' [18] in explaining how many of the Delvin people were forced to oppose her father, saying, 'There were people long ago who didn't want to go at all but they had to do it; they wouldn't be there at all – they were very great with my father – but they were made go.'

Nellie also stressed that the parish priest was friendly with the Weldons. He was close to some of James Weldon's aggressors too, however, for he sat on the new hall* committee with Fr Cogan, his curate, Joseph Clyne, Patrick Corcoran and Patrick Kearney [19] – all key figures in the victimization of James Weldon and his son.

Asked if the characters in the book were based on real people, Nellie replied, 'If the cap didn't fit them, they needn't wear it.'

---

*St Patrick's Hall, built in 1918.

Ballinvalley School, Delvin

FOUR

THE BOYCOTT

He had been some sort of a wild lunatic of a man, but he had written a whole
lot for the stage, and it seemed as if they had to dance now to the tune that he
had played with his life. There were moments now when it seemed that ... this
was going to be an acted summer all the way ... Aren't they living in this
country, anyway, where it's one long Abbey play from one end of the year to
another, day after day, night after night.[1]

In 1918 Ballinvalley (Male) National School (Westmeath 931 in
National Education Office records) had an average of thirty enrolled
students. When Master Weldon arrived at his place of employment on
29 May, the morning after the burning of his son's book, he found
seven pupils there, along with the assistant teacher. Three armed
members of the Royal Irish Constabulary were posted at the gateway.
Soon a crowd of around seventy people marched up, almost everybody
in the village except for Fr Tuite and John Bray. A few had been almost
forced from their homes, according to some accounts. The *Westmeath
Examiner*, stating that certain Cloughan Clubmen were included in
the group, said that a deputation entered the school and, claiming to
be acting on Fr Tuite's instructions, demanded that James Weldon
resign and vacate the building at once.[2] Weldon refused to move and
sought proof of the school manager's backing. A study of reports
suggests that Joseph Clyne issued the directions and was supported by
Halpin, Corcoran 'and a man named Cully'.[3] Clyne was a tall, hefty,
formidable man who weighed over sixteen stone. Even when he knelt
in church, the other parishioners 'looked like children about him'.[4] On
the insistence of the local RIC sergeant, Patrick Rody, they sent for Fr
Tuite, who arrived in an agitated state and warned James Weldon that
if the children did not return he would have to be dismissed. The
schoolmaster retorted that this was not in accordance with the
Maynooth Resolution. (The first Maynooth Resolution of 1894, adopted by the bishops of Ireland, stipulated that three months' notice of

dismissal could not be served on a teacher by a Catholic clerical manager without the bishop's consent – the teacher having the right to be heard in his own defence.[5]) Despite this, the priest issued the three months' notice, then, asking the people to disperse, ordered the assistant and pupils out of the school and locked the door.

> There was little further development till next day [Thursday], though it seems from the time of the visit of the crowd to the school on Wednesday morning, Mr Weldon was under police protection.[6]

The 'further development' alluded to here is not clear. It may refer to the fact that Bishop Gaughran, contacted by Fr Tuite, forbade Weldon's dismissal; or to a Corpus Christi procession in Delvin on Thursday 30 May. It was normal for the principal teacher of Ballinvalley to marshal the boys at this annual show of religious fervour, during which the Blessed Sacrament was held aloft in a golden monstrance and carried through the street, followed by praying parishioners. Positions of authority, stewarding and the like, were cherished and often handed down from one generation to the next. The functions of all teaching staff were clearly recognized. Just as they were expected to take Sunday catechism class for no extra remuneration, so too their duties at the procession were beyond question. James Weldon was snubbed in the 1918 procession, and two of his adversaries, Patrick Kearney, grocer, and Patrick Corcoran, farmer, looked after the Ballinvalley schoolboys instead. Some reports claim that an assistant teacher had been asked to take the children and, not wishing to take the place of a boycotted colleague, she pleaded having to go to Kilbeggan for the day. On her return that night her pony-trap was smashed.

Parishioners were surprised and shocked when at Masses on Sunday 2 June it was announced that Ballinvalley School would reopen the following morning, Fr Tuite stating from the pulpit, 'Wrong steps have been taken which we must redress.' Immediate attempts were made to encourage, cajole or intimidate parents into keeping their children away from Ballinvalley, and transport to other schools in the area was arranged. The plans were successful, and only ten boys turned up for schooling on Monday, most of these from homes of the local workhouse staff. A few more returned during the week but on 4 June James Weldon made a formal complaint to the police about the affair.[7] The *Westmeath Examiner* of the time claimed that within a fortnight thirty boys were back but subsequent averages recorded indicate that, if this was so, they did not remain.

Under The Criminal Law and Procedure Act of 1887 a list of Proclamations and Orders suppressing Sinn Féin organizations came into force on 14 June 1918,[8] but Cloghan Club at this time was more concerned with the Weldon affair. Brinsley MacNamara had been a popular member who often addressed their meetings. Michael Fox, its leader, expelled those who became actively involved in the harassment of the schoolmaster and a statement issued at a county Volunteer meeting in Mullingar warned that action would be taken against members participating in the dispute.

The small community was alive with rumour and innuendo. As pickets were placed on roads leading to the school, there were allegations that Sergeant Rody had been bribed. Brinsley MacNamara was threatened with kidnapping and expulsion. Those who felt libelled by *The Valley of the Squinting Windows* sought legal advice. The local curate, Fr J. J. Cogan, approached parishioners seeking a solution. Some were still convinced that James Weldon had a hand in writing the book or in feeding his son material; others just vented their bitterness on him because Brinsley was not around. Parishioners told Cogan to write to Mr E. A. Shaw, a Mullingar solicitor, instructing him to take an action against James Weldon and his author-son for criminal libel. The plan was to drop the action if Weldon disavowed the book, as he had already agreed to do (in writing, according to one source). Cogan later spoke with Weldon and as a result of the conversation the schoolmaster wrote a letter to Fr Tuite denying connection with the authorship or publication of the book and apologizing for any slight caused.[9] Fr Cogan circulated the letter and also read it from the altar at Mass on Sunday 7 July. He added that the dispute was settled and advised parents to send their children back to school. Things improved for a day or two but the initiative lost momentum and the boycott was resumed fully.

Meanwhile the Weldon family suffered humiliations as they attempted to go about their daily business. They were refused service in most Delvin shops and when Tierneys continued to serve the family, many of their other regular customers asked for their 'book' (in which accounts were kept). Tierneys, while apologetic, were forced to stop trading with the Weldons. Remaining loyal to the distressed family, Tom Lenihan devised a scheme to supply them with foodstuffs. He and his family would purchase extra provisions in a number of shops and, after dark, some of the Weldon children would be sent across the fields to Ellenstown to collect the goods. When the ruse was discovered, the Fitzsimons joined the Corcorans in refusing grazing rights to Tom Lenihan.

Brinsley MacNamara considered emigration to England before deciding finally to seek refuge in Quin, Co. Clare, the home of his future wife. Knowledge of everything he did got back to the parochial house in Delvin, where Fr Tuite, incensed by the book itself and by its repercussions in his parish, had now turned completely against the Weldons. Instead of abating, the storm blew stronger. Meetings about the affair were held on Tuesdays and Thursdays and an 'official' meeting was held every Sunday under Fr Tuite's chairmanship.

> It was indeed pleasant for any stranger to come into Garradrimna now and to behold the delight, as it were, upon its whole face, even from afar off. It would almost seem to the stranger with an inquiring mind, as if a National Movement for the propagation of laughter had been inaugurated in Garradrimna.[10]

Benedict Kiely recalls meeting a man in a bar in Collinstown, five miles west of Delvin, who assured him that a popular Sunday pastime during the years after the book-burning consisted of cycling to Delvin to see the places and people that the book was said to describe. There was even the chance of observing a fight or squabble between supporters and enemies of the Weldons. Local lore supports the sightseeing suggestion but not the fighting. Delvin was being held up to ridicule as more and more people heard about the boycott and other antics in the Garradrimna of Westmeath. Mai Savage was a young girl of about fourteen then, living in Tullamore. She was fond of reading and a schoolteacher friend lent her a copy of *The Valley of the Squinting Windows* with dire warnings of the consequences if she were discovered reading it. The young teacher was terrified of what the local clergy would do if they learned that she possessed a copy. After reading the book Mai went to confession immediately to shrive herself of the dreadful sin she had committed!

Maunsel and Co., the cautious Dublin publishing house, had

printed a thousand copies of MacNamara's book (2000 was their normal run). Hearing about events in Delvin and fearing reprisals, they withdrew the title and made no further effort to have it reviewed or publicized.

An American edition, with a foreword by the author on the Delvin events, was published in 1919 by Brentano of New York. MacNamara wrote of the probability of finding in every Irish farmhouse of the time a copy of *Knocknagow* by Charles Kickham. A stranger, he said, would be inclined to believe that the story of Matt the Thresher must be one of the great books of the world:

> Yet for all the expectations which might be raised up in one by this most popular, this typical Irish novel, it is most certainly the book with which the new Irish novelist would endeavour to contrast his own. For he would be writing of life, as the modern novelist's art is essentially a realistic one, and not of the queer, distant, half pleasing, half saddening thing which could make one Irish farmer's daughter say to another at any time within the past forty years:
>
> 'And you'd often see things happening in real life like in "Knocknagow." Now wouldn't you?'[11]

The things that were happening in Delvin, meanwhile, would never have been countenanced by Norah Lahy or her gentle contemporaries. The boycott of James Weldon's school continued and traders still refused to supply goods to the family. The teacher needed a motor car to travel to his mother's funeral but this was refused him. This treatment continued through 1919 and towards the end of the year another attempt was made to have him removed from the school. This time the curate, Fr Cogan, was involved. On 19 October, when the priest visited the school, James Weldon spoke harshly to him and Fr Tuite reported this to the National Education Office. The Commissioner of National Education severely reprimanded Weldon, warning him that any similar misconduct would 'be visited with a serious penalty'.[12]

> The function of the Irish novelist to evoke reality has been proved in the case of *The Valley of the Squinting Windows*. Upon its appearance the people of that part of Ireland with whom I deal in my writings became highly incensed. They burned my book after the best medieval fashion and resorted to acts of healthy violence. The romantic period seemed to have been cut out of their lives and they were full of life again. The story of my story became widely

exaggerated through gradually increasing venom and my book, which had been well received by the official Irish Press [*sic*] whose reviewers generally read the books they write about, was supposed by some of my own people to contain the most frightful things. To the peasant mind, fed so long upon unreal tales of itself, the thing I had done became identified after the most incongruous fashion and very curiously with an aspect of the very literary association from which I had sprung. Language out of Synge's 'Playboy of the Western World' came to my ears from every side during the days in which I was made to suffer for having written *The Valley of the Squinting Windows.*

'And saving your presence, sir, are you the man who killed your father?'
'I am, God help me!'
'Well then, my thousand blessings to you!' [13]

In quoting this exchange, MacNamara, like Christy Mahon, may have been revelling in the Puckish glory of notoriety. Yet he was relatively untouched by the reaction of the Delvin community, unlike his father who bore the brunt of their harsh treatment. The average attendance at his school for the year 1919 was 17.7. This compared with an average of 36 in 1917 and 30 in 1918. A slight improvement during 1920 brought the average up to 20 but it was back down to 17.7 in 1921 and by 1922 had fallen to 13.4. The National Education Office took action and proposed the amalgamation of the male and female schools (the latter having 47 on the roll).

After his installation in 1906 the Bishop of Meath, Dr Lawrence Gaughran, burned the diocesan archives, thus destroying valuable records of the Land War (1879-1903), a three-phase struggle against landlords by tenants led by the Land League, and of Charles Stewart Parnell's (1846-91) attempts as leader of the Irish Party at Westminster to win Home Rule for the Irish people. No current correspondence of his episcopate (1906-28) survived either, but some individuals have preserved valuable evidence of developments in the Ballinvalley School case. This discloses that J. A. McMahon, a school inspector despatched to investigate and report on the proposed amalgamation of the boys' school with the girls', advised against it. He outlined the history of the affair and the Delvins' view of *The Valley of the Squinting Windows* as a libel on the village and locality. Stressing the decline in averages, he offered his opinion that if amalgamation took place the girls would not be sent to school by their parents and that consequently the staff and pupils of their school would suffer gravely. A case was shortly to come before the lawcourts and, given the strained relations this obviously caused between James Weldon and the local people, McMahon foresaw no chance of settlement until the suit was over, and felt that a decision on the matter should be postponed until then.

Conscious of the hardship his book was causing his father, Brinsley MacNamara wrote (from 11 Iona Drive, Glasnevin, Dublin) to Professor Michael Hayes, Minister for Education, on 2 August 1922. Under Department regulations, the drop in averages would bring about a decrease in salary and subsequent pension, so the author referred to the 'circumstances of [James Weldon's] position for the past four years ... which are now, I believe, about to result in his immediate and complete victimisation'.[14] He mentioned his father's long and faithful service of forty years' teaching in two schools within Delvin parish and even explained his own *nom de plume* as originating from 'the other side' of his family (see p. 21). For the reaction to his book he blamed a section of the Volunteers which, he said, attempted to use the organization to attack his father and the remainder of his family. Alluding to the 'pro-book and anti-book parties', Brinsley attributed credit for restoring law and order not to the RIC, who he claimed were won over by the mob, but to the main body of the Volunteers. The continuing boycott, combined with the dwindling population in what had been a large ranching district, had brought the school average below the minimum needed to maintain his father's salary in his particular grade. The trauma had also affected James Weldon's health, making his position more difficult still. His father, Brinsley pointed out, was within a year or two of retirement and his pension prospects were unfavourable unless special allowances could be made. He appealed for consideration in the matter. None was forthcoming and his father's salary dropped from £338 to £255 with effect from 1 January 1923.

On 12 February 1923 Brinsley MacNamara again wrote to the Department, this time using headed Saorstát Éireann notepaper. (MacNamara did some editorial work from 5 Parnell Square, Dublin for Desmond Fitzgerald, whom he had formerly assisted editing the War of Independence underground news-sheet, *The Bulletin*.) The letter stated that his father's salary had by then been reduced and that the continuing boycott was tantamount to forcing a resignation. He asked what was intended with regard to James Weldon's pension, and for notification of the full extent of the likely loss, explaining that he needed the information in order to instruct a solicitor in an action against the conspirators.

On 10 April 1923 a writ of summons was issued by James Weldon against Fr Tuite and others for 'damages instanced by reason of the conspiracy of the defendants, their agents and servants to injure the plaintiff in his occupation as schoolteacher and being a malicious combination to boycott the school'. Defendants were also alleged to have conspired to deprive him of his salary and so curtail his pension.

* * *

As well as handling his father's case, Brinsley MacNamara was busy with literary work, writing numerous papers and articles for the *Weekly Freeman*, the *Irish Statesman*, the *Irish Weekly Independent*, *The Shamrock*, *The Gael* and *The Dublin Magazine*. On 11 March 1919 his first play, *The Rebellion in Ballycullen*, a three-act work set in the midlands, was produced at the Abbey Theatre. Joseph Holloway was on the warpath:

> 'It wasn't a play at all' said Frank Hugh O'Donnell to T.C. Murray in the vestibule. The author had been called. 'It fell to pieces after Act One' was Sydney Morgan's opinion. 'It was full of clever satirical sayings which the audience took good humouredly, but no amount of clever sayings will make a play without construction and human dramatic incident,' said Murray and added, 'It was ... woefully badly acted ... the prompter had a big part.'

Holloway met MacNamara on 26 March and advised him to rewrite his play, introducing one of the villagers to give their point of view. As in all his writings the diarist sounds pompous when he adds:

> drama arises out of a clash of ideas ... there is none in *Rebellion in Ballycullen* [but it] reads well. Mac, as he sat in front of the fire, his big frame all of a heap in the chair, looked the picture of massive helplessness and dull heaviness. Occasionally he lapses into long silences as he gazes at the fire – a strange, heavy mannered man.

On 23 June 1920, in Clooney church, Quin, Co. Clare, John Weldon, with an address at 17 Hume St, Dublin, married local girl Helena (referred to as Lena hereafter) Degidon, whom he had met when she was teaching in Ballinvalley Girls' School. So the daughter of Patrick Degidon and his late wife, Annie (Forde) of Rylane, became part of a family which was moving towards the climax of five years of strife. Lena had left Delvin in 1913 to take a teaching appointment in Corkscrew Hill, Co. Clare, then accepting another in her home town of Quin. She came to war-torn Dublin where a son, Oliver, was born on 16 May 1921, but was to return to Quin, having decided to settle into peaceful village life for good. There the boy was reared and saw his father only on occasion, when Brinsley's visits, via Athenry to the local station, caused great excitement. One Christmas he fell asleep on the train and awoke in Galway, missing the festivities; but instead he brought Lena and Oliver to Dublin to enjoy a holiday. Another year Brinsley developed a bad dose of rheumatic fever in Quin. With plenty of time to talk and listen, he heard of the temper of the local schoolmaster, who inflicted such punishment that Lena sometimes had to tear up sheets to bandage the wounds of her charges. Compared with him, his father seemed a paragon.

*   *   *

Also in 1920 *The Irishman*, MacNamara's second novel, was published, as was *In Clay and in Bronze*. They were one and the same book. The former, by 'Oliver Blyth', was published by E. Nash, a London house. It has been suggested that they requested the new pseudonym because of the 'Squinting Windows' controversy. *In Clay and in Bronze* used the Brinsley MacNamara pen-name.* The novel was given an early form of marketing. 'A New Book by an author whose first novel was one of the literary sensations of last year,' an order form proclaimed. The advertised price was six shillings and four pence, cheap for 'a remarkable psychological analysis' which promised 'a subtle criticism of Irish Literary and Political Movements' as well as an extraordinary story.

> It was seldom that anyone laughed in Glannidan, but they were always grinning. He saw the tragedies wherein one man or woman was made to

---

* For a planned earlier edition of this work, which never materialized, Mícheál Mac-Liammóir designed a dust-jacket for a fee of one guinea; it was the actor's first design commission.

possess a little nobility of soul and he felt that this was really a lie for in that part of Ireland that he knew he had never experienced such a thing ... He was one of themselves, and his vivid literary expression in terms of life the publication of them before the world ... Perhaps Brian Doyle would attempt an attack upon the book for the *Ballycullen Gazette*. It would abound in all the well-worn phrases which made up his style ... 'An outrage upon all creeds and classes,' 'parishioners, respectable people are implicated.' 'A cold blooded attack upon the Irish peasant and upon holy Ireland.' [15]

If, as has been suggested, MacNamara wrote *In Clay and in Bronze* before *The Valley of the Squinting Windows*, but had the latter published first in protest against his father's ill-treatment by the Delvins, then there is some basis for the accusations made against him. Regarded as autobiographical, *In Clay and in Bronze* depicts rural Ireland and the theatre circles of Dublin and New York. Instead of the Garradrimna of *Windows* we have Glannidan (there is a townland near Delvin called Glenidan) and a similar portrayal of faults and frailties in a small community. However, its publication by Brentano's in New York aroused no controversy.

In an appreciation of Brinsley MacNamara, written for *The Dublin Magazine* in July 1929, Andrew E. Malone (pseudonym of Laurence P. Byrne, author of *The Irish Drama 1896-1928* [London 1929] and later drama critic of *The Irish Times*) wrote of Martin Duignan's story:

[It] is essentially the story of thousands of lads similarly placed in contemporary Ireland. Aspire as they may, these lads are held in the soil; the sticky clay clings to them, clogging their every effort at freedom and damming the intellect which is within them. In a sense [it is] the story of modern Ireland – perhaps ... the story of every peasant lad throughout the world who makes efforts to get free from the soil in which his roots are imbedded as if he were a plant.

Maunsel's published *The Clanking of Chains* in 1920. If anything, given the times, it ought to have created far more of a stir than *The Valley of the Squinting Windows*, with its satirical exposé of verbal patriots and assault on the cap-tipping inferiority complexes of the Irish peasant:

Always the chains clank; the chains which are forged by Irishmen for themselves as well as those which are the residue of prolonged political subjection ... [a] man who was compelled to leave his native village because he would not conform with the mean standards of his neighbours.[16]

The man who twelve years previously had strutted Delvin's court-house stage as Robert Emmet now disregarded the terrible beauty of pure purple patriotism. On its fair features, MacNamara the realist recorded the warts of avarice, the blemishes of vindictiveness, the moles of malice and the boils oozing a purulent discharge of spiteful, covetous, gossiping parochialism:

> It was hard enough to have to listen to them always, but it's something hellish to hear them talking of dying for Ireland.[17]

Anticipating *Juno and the Paycock* by four years, MacNamara's depiction of Ballycullen is echoed in Juno's call:

> Sacred heart of the Crucified Jesus, take away our hearts o' stone ... an' give us hearts o' flesh... Take away this murdherin' hate ... an' give us Thine own eternal love!

As Benedict Kiely remarked:

> In *The Clanking of Chains*, Ballycullen is a scabrous shell around the life of a young man inspired by heroic visions of sacrifice for national independence. Since no good can survive in Ballycullen, and since Ballycullen is made a testing-point for the patriotic temperature of Ireland, the ultimate flight of the young man could only be successful if it led him to a new world without profiteers or rogues or malicious village gossips.[18]

On 30 November 1920 another play by MacNamara opened at the Abbey. 'Owing to numerous complaints the Management insist that ladies sitting in the stalls shall remove their hats,' warned the prog-ramme for *The Land for the People*. This time Brinsley was given an impressive cast. Barry Fitzgerald played Eugene Cooney, and Sean Glynn, a leader of the people, was played by F. J. McCormick (Peter Judge); Michael J. Dolan was 'another leader of the people'.[19] The editor of the *Evening Herald*, J. J. Rice, using the pen-name 'Jacques', called the work 'a demonstration of meaningless motion in monoton-ous manner', then, abandoning alliteration, said he had rarely witnessed such a series of senseless entries and exits. He criticized F. J. McCormick who held a bottle of stout in one scene: 'Not once did he sip the sweetness of the colleen's lips, not once did he sip the softness of the beverage froth.' And Holloway wrote to Frank Fay: 'The author, I fear, hasn't the dramatic gift.'

A fourth novel, *The Mirror in the Dusk*, appeared in Dublin in 1921.

The mists of the morning had lifted and the sun now shone down straight and clear upon the wet, dirty street where the fair was being held. The cattle looked bedraggled, and the men looked bedraggled, all mud and dirt and dung. Thus fell a great drabness with the flowing of the light.[20]

In his *Dublin Magazine* feature Malone pronounced it the best of the author's works to date:

Here indeed is the dreamer dreaming back into his own childhood, and finding it lovely. This novel has ... achieved for its author the praise of the most discerning critics in the press in Great Britain, and it is safe to say that nothing they have said overpraises the great merits of a very notable novel ... As [four children] grow to adult age the shadow of the land falls across their lives, and they are scattered. One to a shop in the town, one to America, one to a loveless marriage. Tragedy grips them all, and even if some of them are what Ballyscurlock calls successes, none of them is permitted to live the life which they would have chosen for themselves were they free from the land-hunger of their elders. Memories of ancient tyrannies cloud their lives from the first, and then competition for the available land kills any neighbourly or Christian feeling which might have developed in them. On almost every page of this novel will be found the essential Ireland of the little farms, of those white-washed cottages which charm the eye of the tourist, and if the inside is not so charming as the colours of the landscape that must not be held against the author, as it is so often done in Ireland, for treachery. Lives, young and old, have been blighted in Ireland in the struggle for land, as lives are being blighted to-day, and as lives will probably continue to be blighted until the land is seen to be just a means of livelihood not superior to other means of subsistence.[21]

This reference to peasant land-hunger is a reminder that some of the bitterness towards James Weldon locally arose from a campaign by an anonymous party to acquire the three-acre plot of land adjoining Ballinvalley School residence (some name James Holmes, who was involved in the 1911 letter incident). The *Westmeath Examiner* had detailed the legal position of parochial landownership in its report of December 1923 and credence is given to this theory by unusually formal correspondence between James Weldon and Fr Tuite about the plot.[22]

In 1922 Brinsley MacNamara faced a crisis of conscience suffered by many young men of his time. Sinn Féin leanings tempted some to oppose the Treaty which followed the Truce in the War of Independence. Others remained loyal to the decision reached on 7

January to ratify the Treaty by a narrow majority of 64 votes to 57 in Dáil Éireann. MacNamara, now becoming more conservative, had opted to support the Treaty.

> While never a revolutionary, [MacNamara] was what most of his generation were – supporters of Arthur Griffith and Sinn Féin. After the Treaty, he was active as a kind of press officer for *Cumann na nGaedheal* and was particularly close to General MacEoin (the former leader of the Longford Brigade).[23]

MacNamara's large and ebullient figure was to become popular on the Dublin literary landscape but according to Michael McDonnell (Irish-American lecturer at Fairfield University, Connecticut), this marked the end of his best period of writing:

> MacNamara was never again to experience years of such generally consistent quality in his work (including a series of twenty-three highly informed articles entitled 'Books and Their Writers' for *The Gael*) as he did in the war-torn period between 1916 and 1922. During this period of rampant Irish nationalism he struggled heroically and alone to tell the truths others would tell in retrospect. The struggle proved too much for one man.[24]

McDonnell also concluded that the author had 'finally become convinced of the ultimate failure of his role as savior' at about that time.

* * *

MacNamara's struggle to save his father continued, however, as the Delvin boycott wore on in a series of malicious occurrences. Many of them stemmed from the visit to Ballinvalley School by Fr Cogan C.C. on Friday 17 October 1919, previously mentioned. In front of the pupils, James Weldon accused the priest of taking boys from the school to serve at High Masses in order to keep down the average. Fr Cogan alleged that Weldon added:

> You are supporting the game and you are the constant companion of the crowd of ruffians and would-be murderers, Clyne, Halpin and Corcoran. You know they are murderers because they made a murderous attack on me and you spend all your time talking to them and you pass by the teachers of the parish without speaking to them, those that did the work in the past. I won't let it go any further. I will report you within a week to the Most Rev. Dr Gaughran.[25]

Fr Cogan informed his parish priest of the incident and then sought counsel from Mullingar solicitor J. J. Macken. He was advised to report the matter formally to Fr Tuite and to state that Weldon, 'in using such language without either justification or provocation, rendered himself liable to instant dismissal and that [Fr Tuite] as manager could forthwith exercise that right'. In his letter to Fr Tuite, the priest alluded to Mr Weldon's threat to write to the bishop, adding, 'I am writing to you so that through you, His Lordship may be made fully cognizant of the facts.' If he was covering himself Fr Tuite was no less careful. On 20 October he wrote to the Secretaries of the Education Board acquainting them of the alleged outburst in Ballinvalley School. They sought further particulars of the event, including a statement from Fr Cogan. Fr Tuite then received a letter from James Weldon; irreverently, perhaps, it was written on black-bordered mourning notepaper. Dated 3 November 1919, it read:

> On full reflection I beg leave to apologize to Father Cogan and am sorry that many annoyances caused me to lose my temper. I have heard you have reported me to the Commissioners [i.e. Education Board] and hope you will now be so good as to withdraw same.[26]

Meanwhile Macken, the Mullingar solicitor, forwarded a copy of Fr Cogan's letter of complaint to the Commissioners; he asked Fr Tuite to send a further copy to Weldon and return to him any statements the teacher wished to make on the matter.

On 1 December 1919 James Weldon wrote a letter to Fr Tuite in which he stated the reasons for his accusation. Only boys from his school, he pleaded, were taken to serve Mass; none of those attending other parish schools because of the boycott was asked. In the curate's presence, he claimed, he asked pupils to verify this and they all admitted to 'some of the priests' asking them.

> He then asked me did I believe that this was done with design, and I replied that in consequence of all I could see of his actions I could come to no other conclusion. I pointed out to him that from the day I was attacked by the mob led by Clyne, Corcoran and Halpin, who did their best to murder me and would have succeeded but for Constabulary being at hand to prevent it, he was constantly in the company of some of the men who took an active part against me, and that as far as I was aware a word of rebuke he never uttered with reference to their conduct or anything they did afterwards in trying to ruin the school.[27]

Weldon went on to complain of saluting the priest and not being acknowledged and of Fr Cogan's ordering boys from the school to go to coursing matches, again depriving the school of their attendance. 'His manner towards me has always been dictatorial and overbearing, frequently insulting, and a word of sympathy he never expressed towards me during the terrible ordeal I have been subjected to for the past year and a half.'

Fr Tuite sent a covering note to the Education Board requesting an immediate investigation to 'dissipate the unworthy aspersions cast on Fr Cogan by the (perhaps disturbed) imagination of Mr Weldon'.[28]

Still under pressure from Fr Cogan's solicitor, the Board were now precipitated into action. On 7 January 1920 they despatched Mr D. J. McEnery, District Inspector, to report on both the boycott in general and the incident involving Fr Cogan. This considerable task involved taking statements from Fr Cogan, James Weldon, Fr Tuite and at least seven parents of children who had left Ballinvalley School and were studying elsewhere.

Many of the interviews covered old ground. Fr Cogan reiterated his version of the incident adding that he actually helped to keep up averages by approaching parents and asking them to return their children to Ballinvalley. He claimed that some complied but took their children away again after a short period. One couple, Patrick and Lucia Kearney, had gone to the trouble of sending their children to a friend in Killucan so that they could attend the local Rathwire school. They claimed that their children were not getting on well at Ballinvalley even before the boycott. At Fr Cogan's request they brought them back to Ballinvalley but said they were forced to remove them again because of the bad language they picked up.

John and Anna Bray, who had sent a child to Collinstown School, stated they had nothing against James Weldon in his treatment of their son although they didn't like him as a teacher because he didn't exercise proper control over the boys' behaviour. Jane and Michael Daly alleged that Weldon called one of their three boys a tramp and wrongly punished another for tearing a book.

Mary Cully was the most outspoken of the witnesses Fr Cogan produced. She had two nephews attending Ballinvalley up to the boycott. 'As a result of the way I was referred to in the Book, I withdrew the boys,' she wrote.[29] Mary Cully worked in Delvin Post Office and equated herself with Garradrimna's 'old bespectacled postmistress, already blinded partially, and bent from constant, anxious scrutiny, poring exultantly over the ... letter in her hand'.[30]

While it would appear that Fr Cogan organized the parents and guardians to support his own account, a pupil, Patrick Tierney, confirmed that he and a boy called Perrick were given a free day by the priest to go to a coursing match but did not do so, going to school instead. In his statement, Fr Cogan admitted that he had given a delicate boy a day off school and permission to go to the match. In response to Weldon's allegation of partisanship, the priest claimed that his relationship with Clyne, Halpin and Corcoran was similar to that which he enjoyed with all his parishioners. Saying that he had arrived in the parish only on 9 May 1918, just before the book-burning incident, he described the MacNamara novel as 'scurrilous and libellous' and said that Fr Tuite was annoyed by it and by what it was doing to Ballinvalley School. He claimed to have done what he could to settle the dispute and, as regards the boycott, he wrote: 'Instead of assisting to keep down the average, I did more than a man's part to keep it up.'

James Weldon agreed in the main with Fr Cogan's statement. He recounted the events of 28 May 1918 and afterwards. Putting his attackers in charge of the procession was a great insult, he protested, as was Fr Cogan's more recent action of giving a young man the task of teaching new altar-boys to serve Mass, traditionally the function of the schoolteacher.

Fr Tuite said that the publication of *The Valley of the Squinting Windows* 'caused madness in the district'. He described Fr Cogan as 'most zealous and anxious for the welfare of the schools ... it was an extraordinary thing on the part of Mr Weldon to attack Fr Cogan in the school'. The parish priest expressed a wish for a change of teacher and said that 'owing to the hostile attitude of the people towards the master, the attendance will never improve in his time'.

Elaborating on this later, Fr Tuite added that even James Weldon's most virulent opponents would wish his departure to be attended by the least possible injury to the interests of himself and his family, but 'on the principle that the teacher is for the school, not the school for the teacher, if one or other is to be sacrificed, surely it is not the school?' In April 1920 James Weldon was severely reprimanded by the Board of Education for his behaviour towards Fr Cogan and was warned that any similar misconduct would be visited with a serious penalty.

* * *

Brinsley MacNamara's published criticism in *The Gael* of 14 November 1921 dwelt on the exaggerated importance given to the Irish Literary Renaissance; Synge's genius in raising the bardic tradition from near-extinction; and the lazy and unimaginative literary criteria applied by rural audiences. The following week, in an article called 'A Certain Kind of Critic. The Ireland of Yesterday. The Disappearance of "Pat" and his Replacement. What the "Realist" really is', Mac-Namara disparaged the anti-realist as savage, mentally elderly and belonging to an Ireland older than the realistic country of the day.* The anti-realist, he contended, is 'the diehard of the hypocrisy of Irish life ... always searching for "brightness" and "beauty"', deploring the lack of these in the writings he criticizes:

> He is really upon the side of romance only to the mean extent that he will not see the Ireland which he and his like, upon the side of the enemy, had made the Ireland of lying and knavery and drunkenness and cowardice and treachery. The Ireland, in short, where Romance was impossible since it would be a lie ... The propagandists who wrote to prolong the gombeen era were not really Irish. Their writing ... followed abjectly in the pseudo-humorous English view of us all down through the nineteenth century.
>
> The idea that such charlatans as Lever and Lover and the silly malignant 'Punch' had created, they were anxious to perpetuate. They were all tremendously anxious to discover the omadhaun and here it must be said that, for reasons implicit in the character of the period itself, it was not difficult to find, about this time, many choice specimens of this particular human species, because as a matter of fact we seriously threatened to become a nation of omadhauns.

---

* Thomas Hardy, Brinsley MacNamara's favourite author whom he frequently invoked, was also immune to Imagists' ideas and although his poetry was romantic in character it too reflected the toughness of experience foreign to Victorian poets of his youth and middle age.

MacNamara saw the Easter Rising of 1916 as putting an end to all romantic thought and action.

> Its martyrs had died for everything that Freedom means, including that of Literature, and [the anti-realist critic's] voice was merely the dying echo of a whinge out of the really un-Romantic Ireland that was dead and gone ... 'Pat' was dead without having left any more heroic tradition behind him than the whirl of his shillelagh which he used, in the interests of his frivolity, to knock his brother 'Pat' on the head.

The killing was a slow process, according to the author, for 'Pat' had attained a position of international importance as a gigantic figure of fun surpassing Sandy the Scot and Taffy the Welshman to take his place alongside John Bull and Uncle Sam. Dare we say that far from dying, 'Pat' has outlived his peers, as evidenced by the abundance of shamroguery on sale for tourists?

MacNamara's opinion may have been influenced by critical reaction to his own work to date. Was it truly realism that left his books devoid of levity? Of course the countryside was dull and depressing, often hungry and ill-cared for, but surely he witnessed some gaiety; the dances at crossroads and in Tom Flynn's barn, for example? 'The barn dances were very popular and people came from the village, Killalon and Archerstown to dance the night away. Music was provided by French fiddles, accordeons and on special occasions Matt Sheridan would play the drums.'[31] Threshing festivities, *céilís* or impromptu sprees were common in the most backward areas. As for 'Pat', were the characters in his later plays not stage Irish? In April 1926 W.B. Yeats wrote to Olivia Shakespear about *Look at the Heffernans!* :

82 Merrion Square
15th April 1926

... At present I am suffering from a play. A certain Irish dramatist a year ago sent us a rather vulgar but highly skilful play which we Directors and the whole theatre hated. We put it on and off. Then at last the evil moment had come and last Monday it was played and now as we feared every seat is taken and at night the streets before the theatre packed with motors. I sat it out in misery and had two furious interviews with the author by telephone. I phoned to the author 'We did your play that you might judge it for yourself. Do you think the degradation of youth a theme for comedy – the comedy of the newspapers?' Every country likes good art until it produces its own form of vulgarity and after that it will have nothing else ... The theme is young women throwing themselves at the heads of horrible old men for marriage ... I have given orders that all the young women are to tousle their heads that we may not mistake them for whole women, but know them for cattle.[32]

As early as 1913 Brinsley had written, 'The halo has fallen from the head of Mr Yeats. His gesture has lost its eloquence. He has put on the garment of the commonplace and dwells among the businessmen of his time' (*Irish Independent*, 9 May 1913). Now, undaunted, the playwright concluded that Yeats, at sixty-one years of age, was upset by the spectacle of senile characters chasing nymphets around the stage.[33]*

There was little comedy, however, in the drama being acted out in Delvin, and the stage was now set for the show-down in Dublin's law-courts where James Weldon, schoolmaster, would take on his clerical manager and others in 'The Case of the Squinting Windows'.

* One playgoer who saw that production considers the work – a knock-about satire on country match-making – was performed vulgarly and cites Harry Brogan's appearance with a couple of fly-buttons undone, which sent the house into hysterics.

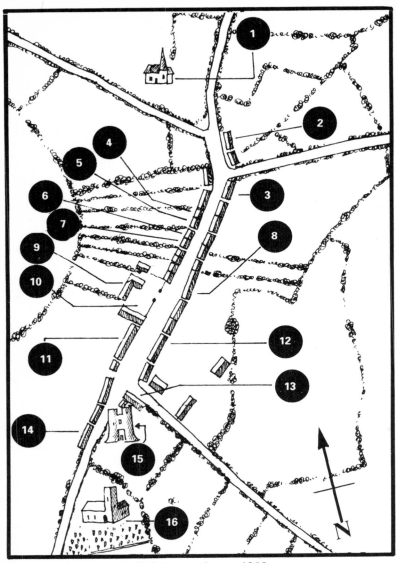

Delvin premises, c. 1918

1. R.C. church
2. Smith's No. 1
3. Smith's No. 2
4. North's
5. Tierney's
6. Clyne's – bar
7. Clyne's – butcher
8. Post office
9. Market House
10. Market square
11. Midland Arms
12. Esperanto Hotel
13. Old courthouse
14. RIC barracks
15. Delvin castle
16. C. of I. church

FIVE

THE TRIAL

they loudly deplored the fact that he did not possess a squinting window even
as each of themselves. Their windows were their very lives, for through them
each looked into the windows of the souls of others, often to the extent of
shattering an enemy through the very vehemence of that long, stony stare.[1]

As 'The Trial of the Squinting Windows' drew near, Brinsley
MacNamara was afforded some relief by the warm reception for his
play *The Glorious Uncertainty*, first produced at the Abbey Theatre on
27 November 1923. It portrays the events surrounding a flapper race-
meeting in the midlands when Gabriel Cunneen is prompted to repair
the failing fortunes of his house by turning amateur bookmaker. It was
given a distinguished cast: Sara Allgood played Julia Cunneen, Eileen
Crowe her daughter; Sam Price was played by Barry Fitzgerald,
Simon Swords by F. J. McCormick. Arthur Shields, Gabriel Fallon
and M. J. Dolan also took part.

Critic J.B.H. in *The Freeman's Journal* found it a 'sparkling comedy'
with 'splendid acting ... an agreeable and welcome experience ... a
particularly good play. Nay, in its most farcical phrases, it is supremely
excellent ... The author was loudly called for.' Even the redoubtable
Joseph Holloway was generous in his praise: 'A winner ... by far the
most workmanlike play Mac has yet written.' Lennox Robinson
thought 'the characterization ... so good and the atmosphere ... so
redolent of the turf that one yields at once to its gay-hearted mood'.[2]
Robinson criticized the story-line as 'too obviously a playwright's
invention', yet some Delvin people in Dublin for the trial went to the
Abbey and thought they saw themselves in it.

James Weldon's solicitors, Malley & Charles of Nassau Street,
Dublin, wrote to the Board of Education seeking Weldon's release
from teaching duties to attend the trial and were told that it was a
matter for the school manager, Fr Tuite. J. J. Macken, acting for Fr
Tuite, sought copies of McEnery's inspection report from the Board,

as well as documentary evidence of the Fr Cogan complaint issue. After initial refusals, he eventually received a copy of the Fr Cogan correspondence but was told that McEnery had left the Department and that, furthermore, his report was confidential. Macken then issued a subpoena for the Secretary of the National Education Office, Padraic O'Bronehan, to attend as witness on behalf of Fr Tuite and bring records and correspondence between the Board and Frs Tuite and Cogan.

Affidavits were sworn before the parties' solicitors; in the main these were technical denials of possession of certain documents. The Writ of Summons was issued on 10 April 1923 'for damages instanced by the Plaintiff by reason of the conspiracy of the Defendants, their Agents and Servants to injure the Plaintiff in his occupation as School Teacher and being a malicious combination to boycott the Plaintiff's school'. Although the trial was set for 16 November 1923, it was not to open until 5 December of that year.

Earlier a strange thing had happened. Brinsley MacNamara was a man who detested lies. Even his enemies, who say he could be caustic or sneering, attest to his integrity. Yet in January 1923 he had written a letter to Fr Tuite that was at best naïve and foolish:

> Ballinvalley, Delvin,
> 21st January 1923.
>
> Sir,
> I have been deputed by the Chief Executive Officer of National Education to interview you in connection with the present condition of Ballinvalley Boys' School and to discuss the matter so that certain arrangements may be made. The Chief Executive Officer of National Education believes you to be the Manager of Ballinvalley School. Your failure to grant me this interview has, however, confirmed me in the well-grounded suspicion that not you but certain persons, to whose illegal actions you have lent your sanctions and complicity, constitute the managing body of Ballinvalley School.
>
> I am still open to be otherwise convinced upon this and notwithstanding the fact that because of your abominable treatment of my people here, it is indeed very distasteful to me to discuss with you any matter whatsoever. I am prepared to meet you at any hour you may name up to 2 p.m. to-morrow, Monday. Failing this, other and most drastic action will be taken so that you may be fully recovered to a sense of your grave responsibilities in the matter.
>
> Yours etc.
> Brinsley MacNamara [3]

Fr Tuite despatched the letter to the Board of Education who, after considerable delay (29 November – a few days before the trial) wrote to Brinsley asking for an explanation, since he had no licence to take such action. No other correspondence on the subject is available but MacNamara's letter seems like an ill-advised and desperate effort to cancel legal proceedings.

The *Midland Reporter* of 6 December gave the court case four headlines: 'Delvin Schoolmaster's £4000 Claim'; 'Conspiracy Alleged against Parish Priest and Seven Others'; 'An Unusual Case from Co. Westmeath'; 'Story of Indignation Meeting and Burning of Son's Book'. A number of Delvins took the train to Dublin from Athboy station. They discussed the latest news of the affair and the rumours that one of the defendants had signed over his property to his wife so that, if convicted, he could plead inability to pay a fine. Tom Lenihan and one of the Duffys had travelled the previous day. A watch needed repairs and they availed of the opportunity to leave it into Jameson's of Lower Sackville Street. When the assistant there was writing down the Delvin address he blurted out his disapproval of the disgraceful book Brinsley MacNamara had written about the place. Next morning Lenihan noticed the same man on the jury panel and informed the defence council of the incident. An objection to his serving on the jury was sustained. In the light of what occurred later, this may have been significant.

Nellie Weldon remembered her mother saying the case should never have been brought to court when there was a priest involved. Wise mother, perhaps, if the story told to Benedict Kiely by the writer Philip Rooney was true:

> Philip was going to Navan races and there was a clergyman with him; they were in the public bar of Crinnion's Hotel. The clergyman had a few drinks taken and he was talking loudly about various matters, you know, ecclesiastical and otherwise. Philip was very gentlemanly; he got a little bit worried for the cleric's sake and he said, 'Father, I think we'll move into the resident's lounge because, you know, if some of those remarks got back to the bishop!'
>
> The decent man said to Philip: 'Philip, no bishop can touch me. I'm the man [who] drilled the witnesses in the Weldon case.'[4]

Research into the court proceedings for this book proved most frustrating. In the State Paper Office, Public Records Office, and certain legal and private archives, the situation was the same: documents relating to the case were indexed, details were followed through, the file was present, but all material relating to the Weldon case was missing. Even archival copies of the *Westmeath Examiner* had been tampered with: the section outlining the result of the action being torn off. My experience in researching various topics, personalities and subjects over the years leads me to believe that documents concerning the Weldon case were removed deliberately.

At the time of the case, it was common practice for newspapers to report proceedings verbatim. The *Westmeath Examiner*, the *Midland Reporter* and *The Irish Times* all carried near-identical coverage. The case opened on 5 December 1923 before Lord Justice O'Connor and a special jury. [5] What follows is a digest of the trial reports from *The Irish Times* of 5 – 8 December:

> The defendants in the case are listed: along with Fr Tuite, these were Michael Cully (farmer); Patrick Halpin (butcher); Joseph Clyne (butcher); Patrick Corcoran (farmer); Thomas Fitzsimons, senior (retired publican); Patrick Kearney (grocer); and John Bray (farmer). They were charged with conspiring to injure the plaintiff in his occupation of schoolteacher by means of a malicious combination to boycott his school, and with loss and damage by intimidation and otherwise; these charges were denied by the defendants. James Weldon was represented by Sergeant Hanna, Mr Jellett KC and Mr Martin Maguire (instructed by Messrs Malley and Charles); Fr Tuite by Mr Lardner KC and Mr Geoghegan (instructed by J. J. Macken); Halpin and Corcoran by Mr Lynch KC Mr Denning and Mr Walsh (instructed by Messrs N.J. Downes and Co.); and Clyne, Kearney, Cully and Bray by Mr Meredith KC, Mr Wood KC and Mr Hamilton (instructed by E.A. Shaw).

> *Day One*
> Sergeant Hanna opened by stating that the plaintiff was seeking £4000 in damages, and went on to give an account of the events of 28 and 29 May. The crowd who approached Weldon at North's shop were, he claimed, about to beat the teacher when the police intervened. Armed police again protected Weldon

from violence at the school the following day. Clyne, one of the main spokesmen, demanded that he resign and leave immediately. The conspiracy was put in force the next week after Fr Tuite's decision to reopen the school. Weldon had apparently been threatened with his son's arrest or kidnap if he failed to withdraw from the school. After three weeks he was forced to sign an agreement that he would apologize. [This is the only mention of written intent to apologize.] At this the judge interjected: 'Apologize for what, Sergeant; for having a son?' to which Hanna replied, 'I suppose that would be it, My Lord.' A promise to withdraw the boycott at this point was not fulfilled, however, and on 22 June Weldon wrote to Fr Tuite saying that he had nothing to do with the publication of the book and disavowing anything distasteful or undesirable in it. This, said Hanna, was done solely to relieve his mind of the terrible strain and in spite of his unwillingness to cringe to the murderous mob which had so savagely attacked him. As regards the Fr Cogan incident, Weldon claimed that he had defended himself and as a result was reported for discourtesy.

Weldon, called to give evidence, asserted that he was generally believed in Delvin to be the author of the book. In response to the judge's comment, 'I suppose you could not write a book like that to save your life,' he said, 'I never wrote a letter to the newspaper even in my life.' Cross-examined by Lynch, he went on to say that he had known nothing of his son's writing the book, the first intimation he got of its publication being from Fr Tuite in mid-May 1918.

[The questioning then took one of its many diversions from a supposed investigation of a conspiracy charge into an attempt to put the book on trial.]

Lynch, having established that Weldon had read the American edition of the *Valley*, asked, 'Does the preface state the characters are taken from real life?' Weldon replied, 'He stated that he wrote from what he saw.' Lynch defended the relevance of further queries on the grounds that he would prove certain people were mentioned in the book. This exchange followed:

LYNCH: Can you point to a single redeeming character in the book except the old schoolmaster?

WELDON: I am not a literary critic and I would not be able to answer you that.

LYNCH: Isn't it a fact that the priests, farmers, traders, and school-teachers, except the old schoolmaster, were all held up to ridicule and contempt in the book?

WELDON: I don't think so.

LYNCH: You would not think it right to describe a clergyman as 'the flirtatious boy of the district'?

WELDON: I did not describe him in any such terms.

[This final answer shows up the general confusion and distortion, with Weldon being asked to explain and defend the work of someone else.]

Tom Lenihan, postman and friend of the Weldons, testified to having seen the teacher being dragged out of North's shop by Halpin, assisted by Clyne. He gave the account quoted earlier (pp. 32-3) of the exchange between Clyne and Tuite at the Parochial House.

Day Two
Patrick Rody, an ex-RIC sergeant, estimated that between forty and sixty people turned up at the school on 29 May. He intervened, ordering them to send for Fr Tuite. In reply to the judge, Rody described the crowd as peaceful but agreed that forty or sixty going into a shop to bring a man out was very curious. In cross-examination Rody said that he had interviewed Weldon on the night of 28 May and saw no mark of an assault on him. He also stated that he had a special police patrol in readiness, giving them instructions to stay about the village that day. [As this would have involved consultation with head-quarters in Castlepollard, it suggests anticipation of trouble.]

John O'Rourke, a police constable, testified to seeing an angry crowd of about thirty-five or forty, including all the defendants except Bray and Fr Tuite, outside Clyne's pub; some of them were under the influence of drink. On reaching North's they rushed in, at some signal from Cully. The police were just behind and O'Rourke saw Clyne and Halpin in grips with Weldon, dragging him along while the crowd shouted, 'Pull him out, pull him out.' O'Rourke got between Clyne and Halpin, shoved Clyne out and got Weldon back into the house. He described the crowd as very threatening; they waited for about five minutes shouting to get back in, till he put his hand on the holster of his revolver and said, 'If you don't get back you will have to take the consequences.' On their return from the Parochial House there was hooting and booing as they passed North's house. He estimated the crowd at the school the following morning at about sixty.

Thomas Heslip, another policeman, claimed that Clyne responded to Rody's remonstrations by saying, 'Weldon should be strung up like a fox for the hounds,' though Rody, recalled later, did not remember this comment. This conveyed to Heslip the meaning that Weldon should be lynched. Lynch provoked laughter by retorting, 'Don't bring the Lynches into it at this stage.' Heslip also attested to having on several occasions protected Weldon's house and escorted him in the village, precautions which were necessary for the greater part of that summer. Thomas Weldon corroborated this account of the family's treatment, giving evidence of having been refused goods in shops until the police came with him. He also testified that his brother had never discussed the book with him, nor had he ever heard of it until it was published.

Patrick Casey, District Councillor at the time, claimed to have been at the head of the crowd going to the school, whose principal object was, he said, peace. He alone of all the defendants gave evidence that it had been arranged to picket the roads to the school. The general opinion was that Weldon had given his son the information written in the book, and people would have been satisfied if he had disavowed it. Casey, who acknowledged the existence of a family quarrel with James Weldon, answered the judge's comments on condemning a man unheard with, 'Well, considering I was described in the book myself.' Asked if he thought his actions were fair, he replied, 'As we knew it at the time, it was fair enough.' He had withdrawn from the others, he said, because they did not support him enough, at which the judge observed, 'I wonder is there much worse said about the people of Delvin in the book than you have said now.'

At the close of the case for the plaintiff, Meredith was granted a direction in favour of John Bray, with costs to be considered afterwards. Similar requests on behalf of Fr Tuite, Halpin and Corcoran were refused. Addressing the jury for Halpin and Corcoran, Lynch commented that the author at least must be delighted with the proceedings, which repaid him for his financial and other assistance to the plaintiff with 'an advertisement that has secured for him, probably for all time, a position that will take him from the obscurity from which he might not otherwise have emerged'. Pointing out that parents were entitled to choose any school they liked for their children, Lynch said there was no evidence of picketing or boycotting. He cast doubt on the assertion that the Weldon family had known nothing of the book until it was published, and defended the indignant reaction of people lampooned and caricatured in it and their right to question Weldon on his involvement. The events of 29 May were of a most harmless kind and those of the 28th an outburst of feeling on the part of the people in Delvin. The plaintiff, he said, had not proved anything that was necessary to prove in order to succeed in his action.

Meredith, who followed, attributed the falling-off in school attendance to war conditions, the closing of the workhouse and barracks in the district, a quarrel between Weldon and Fr Cogan, Weldon's illness and his vindictive treatment of pupils. [He does not seem to have been asked to explain why various factors should suddenly combine to produce an overnight drop of more than twenty pupils.]

Fr Tuite gave evidence that a crowd of about twenty came to his door on 28 May, impassioned to get rid of Weldon. Tuite pointed out that it was not easy to get rid of a teacher, to which one replied: 'We will hunt him.' Weldon promised the priest to write a statement saying that he had nothing to do with the authorship of the book. In response to the judge's question,

'Did you think it was unjust to visit the sins of the son upon the father?' Tuite said, 'There is something unjust about it.'

Day Three

Fr Cogan, who on 9 May had been appointed to the parish with the school specifically put under his charge, stated that shortly before 28 May he got to know there was trouble in the parish. [This, with Rody's evidence, confirms foreknowledge of trouble.] Cogan attested to the common belief that Weldon was the author of the book but denied the existence of a boycott, admitting only to public indignation, which he did his best to put down. He refuted the suggestion that he had asked Weldon to sign a statement, saying that his son would be arrested otherwise. He had, he said, arranged an agreement between the teacher and the villagers whereby Weldon would write a letter to Fr Tuite disavowing all connection with the publication and authorship of the book and the villagers would withdraw legal proceedings against him and his son. When the letter arrived Cogan was instructed by the defendants and others to write to E. A. Shaw, solicitor, of Mullingar, withdrawing the action of criminal libel against James and John Weldon.

The next witness was Joseph Clyne, who stated that the book had given great offence (the judge observing that the truth sometimes gave offence). Clyne described leaving the church on 28 May and joining a crowd on the way to Fr Tuite's. On passing North's someone suggested bringing Weldon out with them to give an explanation. Clyne went over to the door and said to Weldon, sitting inside, 'There is a deputation going down to Fr Tuite over this book which we believe you and your son wrote —' He was interrupted when Weldon, rising and raising his stick, tried to assault him. Clyne denied catching Weldon by the throat and claimed that he would have been seriously assaulted had not Halpin caught the stick. He also denied speaking at the Parochial House and addressing the Market Square meeting, asking people to go to the school the next morning. He had not called for recruits for picketing; nor, to his knowledge, had anyone else. As regards the alleged statement that Weldon should be strung up like a fox for the hounds, he said that he never used his tongue in such a way. In the scene at the school on 29 May he had neither informed Weldon that he had been sent by Tuite nor driven out the children and assistant teacher. He described following Tuite into the school and hearing Weldon say: 'This is a nice state of affairs the Brannagans and the Shannons have brought on.' Replying to the judge he said that these were names given in the book. He had heard no mention of dismissal or notice at the school, and denied all allegations of subsequent conspiracy, intimidation and obstruction. On Clyne's putting the number at the school at about thirty-five or forty, the judge said: 'If you are ever sending a deputation to any of the Ministers in Merrion Street, it should be more limited in number,' causing laughter in the court.

Halpin, following, gave a similar account of the events of 28 May; he denied trying to drag Weldon into the street and confirmed Clyne's account of Weldon's attempted assault and his own intervention. He too asserted his innocence on all picketing charges. Cully, Corcoran and Kearney did likewise, with Cully adding that he thought the whole thing was over on 7 July 1918 [when Weldon's letter to Fr Tuite was read out at Mass in Delvin]. Thomas Fitzsimons, the remaining defendant, was ill and unable to attend the trial.

Mrs Merriman then testified that no one had ever asked her to withdraw her children from the school, and that when, at Fr Cogan's request, she had brought them back, Weldon said: 'You brought them back because you had to. You can bring them back to your drunken husband.' [Weldon was later to deny that this had ever happened but Hanna at this point seemed tacitly to admit it and seek to explain, saying Mrs Merriman did not know that her husband had headed a deputation to the workhouse to have the children there removed from the school.]

Evidence was then heard that Weldon had beaten pupils. One witness, Michael Daly, claimed that the teacher had beaten his younger brother and, when his older brother complained, called them tramps; they had gone home and not been allowed to return. [Again a suggested motive is implied here by Jellett's comment that the witness did not remember any meeting in his father's house, or seeing Clyne, Halpin or any of the other defendants there.]

This closed the case for the defendants.

Weldon was then recalled and gave the average attendances at the school between January 1916 and December 1922. His salary had diminished by £161 and his loss on the capitation grant would be £14. The loss in pension, if the 10 per cent reduction were taken into consideration, would be £72 a year. Replying to Hanna, Weldon contradicted Fr Cogan, saying that the document he signed, which apologized for offence given by the book, had been dictated by the curate, who told him that his son would be arrested if he failed to sign. Cogan also assured him he would see to it that the children were sent back to the school. There was, said Weldon, no question whatever of legal proceedings being brought against him or his son. He also denied the allegations of beatings. On Weldon saying that publication of the book had been stopped by letter, the judge enquired whether this remained the case. Lynch replied that the ban was lifted after these proceedings.

Counsel for the defendants addressed the jury, contending that there was no evidence of conspiracy. The judge made a distinction between Tuite and the other defendants, saying that he thought the priest stood differently from the rest and was not in the movement against the teacher.

Day Four

Meredith delivered a summing-up to the jury on behalf of Clyne, Kearney and Cully, followed by Jellett on behalf of Weldon. Meredith described the evidence as proving only that there had been an 'epidemic of indignation' in Delvin against James Weldon and his son. The events of 28 May were, he said, spontaneous; the people involved were respectable and not of the criminal type. If the alleged assault was taken out of the case, no illegal action was suggested against them. On 29 May the crowd went to get a disclaimer from Weldon that this book had anything to do with Delvin, wanting the message to go to the people of Ireland that there was no gross immorality going on in the town of Delvin, and that the people there were not like the characters portrayed in the book. Weldon was to disavow the authorship as well as the suggestions in the book; this, said Meredith, he would have done at once if he had had the sense of a tom-tit, and that would have been the end of it. Weldon, however, was an obstinate man and had taken up a fighting attitude at once. He ended by reiterating the alleged causes for the drop in attendance – war conditions, etc.

Jellett, closing for Weldon, referred to his long and creditable career as a teacher and his previously cordial relations with the Delvin villagers. The people who joined the crowd on 28 and 29 May were all out for the same purpose, clear from the statement reported by Fr Tuite: 'We will hunt him.' The theory advanced by the defendants was, said Jellett, blown to pieces by the priest's testimony that the dispute was going on to the present moment. He criticized Tuite, both in his capacity as parish priest and as school manager, for not taking a firm stand against the actions of the defendants. The total loss to James Weldon in the figures put down was about £1740 but the jury was urged not to confine damages to that amount, given the plaintiff's present position as outcast in the village. If this sort of thing was allowed to go on, ended Jellett, there would be no real social life in Ireland.

Justice O'Connor then addressed the jury, reminding them that the main question was whether there had been a conspiracy to boycott. [The jury may indeed have needed reminding of this fact, given the side-tracking of the trial into attacks on the book, justifications of the villagers' actions and allegations against Weldon.] If there was a conspiracy to secure Weldon's dismissal, said the judge, then the plaintiff had suffered no loss on that behalf as he had never been dismissed. He went on to the question of John Weldon's having given financial assistance to his father in this action. [This may have been something which attracted comment or criticism, given that Lynch had referred to it earlier.] The judge defended the author's right to provide such support.

Some reference to the book was, he stated, essential, both from the plaintiff's and the defendants' points of view; the former had to suggest some motive for the defendants' conduct towards him, and the latter insisted that it gave great offence, with the result that they were up in arms against it. Extended references, however, were not relevant; without scrutinizing the book and then the lives of every person mentioned in it the jury could not know whether it was a good book or a bad one, true or false. [Here, as elsewhere in the trial, Justice O'Connor seems to accept that actual villagers are portrayed in the novel.]

He commented on the Irish proneness to be led and suggested that in this instance Casey might have been the agitator. The case rested on what the jurors believed the object of the defendants to be in the events of 28 and 29 May: to prevent Weldon functioning in his school or to approach him as a peaceful deputation and ask whether he was responsible for the book. He went on to deride the idea of thirty or forty men being described as a deputation and to stress the importance of Casey's evidence. [This makes his own position seem fairly clear.] If they accepted his testimony that an agreement was made at the open-air meeting to boycott the school, it was very hard to avoid the conclusion that there had been a conspiracy. The attendance at the school had dropped from 43 to 13.7 and the defendants, if guilty, would be liable as long as the results of the conspiracy lasted. The judge expressed his sympathy for Fr Tuite, a very old man put in a position of extreme difficulty: there was, he said, no evidence against him. If the plaintiff was right, he concluded, he was entitled to substantial damages.

The jury, after an absence of forty minutes, failed to agree. They were directed to find a verdict for Bray, entering costs, and were then discharged.

* * *

'There are certain situations in life,' he began, 'which are almost too deep for words. The present is such a situation … there is nothing left for me but to give him his walking papers.'[6]

Brinsley MacNamara had prepared a brief and stood by to give evidence, but he was not called. The *Evening Herald* made the case its lead story for four days, contributing further details of the testimony. It reported James Weldon's description of Fr Tuite coming to the school, holding up his hand and saying, 'I dismiss you, you are no use to me any longer,' at which the judge remarked, 'When you say he held up his hand, was it in benediction or in surrender to a superior force?' He drew laughter from the crowded public gallery. There was also further elaboration of His Lordship's summing-up:

> There ought to be a bit of give and take in these matters ... They had for such a long period of time been holding themselves up – and rather unsuccessfully – as a country unparalleled in sanctity and scholarship that he was afraid their national character was in some danger of degeneration, and he was afraid he himself, and some other people as well, used to wish there never had been a saint or scholar in Ireland (laughter). At any rate their national conceit had got some little knock in the last few years and perhaps they would all be the better of it when they came to face the actual facts of life in this country.

The *Irish Independent* felt 'It was a pity, after so much expense had been incurred' that the jury failed to agree. It was said that this happened because of just one man holding out in favour of James Weldon.* With Philip Rooney's story in mind, was this one man the substitute juror, and were more than the witnesses in the case drilled?

When John Bray came home with his ninety pounds in costs, the money was taken from him by the boycott committee to help offset expenses. (This and transport details suggest that the whole operation was tightly organized.)

The ubiquitous Joseph Holloway was present in Court 4; he may have relished the drama of the occasion but his diary was mainly concerned with the theatre personalities who joined him in the gallery. His abiding impression was the feebleness of the parish priest, Fr Tuite, and how little he remembered. He wrote:

> One always heard of the sins of a father being visited on his children; but here is a case that the supposed sin of his son was visited on his father.[7]

His words were to be echoed in critical comment for generations. Literary Dublin was piqued but there was no surge of protest on behalf of freedom of expression. With unintentional irony, the *Westmeath*

---

* Before 1967 a jury verdict had to be unanimous.

Examiner of 8 December placed a report on 'Those "Squinting Windows" – and that "Valley"' alongside its leading article, headed: 'Freedom of Speech'. Alas, the editorial was referring to 'persons in this country who at Election times endeavour to prevent any but their own side from getting a hearing'.

Some forces, however, gathered in the cause of an artist's right to present things as he saw them, to base fiction upon fact. Realizing that James Weldon and Brinsley MacNamara had suffered financially and were in no position to have the case reopened, a group organized an appeal for funds (see circular, p. 78). Among them were W. B. Yeats, George Russell (AE), Oliver St John Gogarty, James Stephens and James Douglas. Hugh McCartan, Secretary of the Appeal Fund Committee, engaged Malley and Charles to prepare an engross appeal. They forwarded to him a draft which had been settled and approved by Sergeant Hanna KC and Mr Jellett KC, both of whom had appeared for James Weldon in the unsuccessful case:

To Hugh McCartan Esq.
4 Gilford Avenue
Sandymount

CONFIDENTIAL
WELDON SUBSCRIPTION FUND

We send you herewith a copy of an appeal issued on behalf of the Weldon Subscription Fund. Lest you may not have seen any report of the case, may we briefly acquaint you with the outstanding points … In 1918 there was published by Messrs Maunsel & Co. a novel entitled *The Valley of the Squinting Windows*. The author of the book, Brinsley MacNamara, is the son of a national schoolteacher at Ballinvalley, Co. Westmeath. On publication of the book, people in the school area took offence to the tone, professing to find themselves and their district unkindly satirised and even caricatured. Because of this and because they alleged that Mr Weldon and not his son, who writes under a pseudonym, was the author of the book, an attempt was made to boycott Mr Weldon and his school and generally to make life impossible for him in the district. As a schoolmaster's income is dependent on the average attendance at his school, this activity reacted very severely on Mr Weldon, whose salary is his only means of livelihood. An action was taken by Mr Weldon in Dublin for alleged conspiracy to boycott, against certain defendants. The case was heard by Lord Justice O'Connor and a special jury, and resulted in a disagreement.

The following are extracts from the Lord Justice's charge:

In the first place, the plaintiff did not write it. In the second place, on his testimony, he did not suggest it; in the third place, according to his evidence, he did not know it was going to be written. So, he is not in any sense responsible unless you are prepared to make the father responsible for everything the son does, rightly or wrongly. But, if I let my human feelings take hold of me so that I go out on the highways and byways and assault and conspire to boycott a man, then this is the place to account for it. If one jumps to a harsh, rash conclusion about another, and acts upon it to the detriment of the other, is it not right that he should pay for the damages? The plaintiffs held that the talk of a deputation was merest nonsense. Thirty or forty men described by Constable O'Rourke as comprising the 'riff-raff of the village' – a deputation! Clyne made the strange suggestion that instead of Weldon being attacked, he attacked them. Weldon was, at any rate, a plucky man and resisted. The police interfered and he escaped with his life by a laneway. The sergeant put it to Clyne that they were after Weldon like hounds after a fox. And what did the hounds do with the fox when they got him? Deputation indeed! It was the funniest kind of deputation he had ever heard of.

Much comment had been made on points which he wrote in a letter and subsequently, that the plaintiff lost his temper. Did the jury wonder at that? If they were there like rats in a trap and the village tyrants were persecuting them and trying to deprive them of their means of livelihood, would they not have fierce anger at such an injustice exercised towards them? The agitation permeated every fibre of the spirit of Delvin. Was not the result of that, that every person knew that this was a 'tainted school' – an expression from the phraseology of the eighties with regard to 'tainted farms'. A nod was as good as a wink. 'You are going to Mr Weldon's school are you?' Such an expression in these circumstances, without any word, would be sufficient to keep the children away.

If the jury held with the Plaintiff, he was entitled to such damages as would vindicate him and prevent a repetition. If they thought so, and did so, they would have vindicated liberty in Delvin and elsewhere, for village tyranny was a terrible thing and more particularly so in the case of a man whose avocation kept him there whether he wished or not.

These extracts from the judge's charge speak for themselves. This fund has been opened not only to assist Mr Weldon to have a new trial and thus obtain reparation for the very serious losses he has sustained, but also to vindicate what, in the opinion of the organizers of this appeal, is a vital principle of cultured society – freedom of thought and speech. Through the father in this case, it is sought to enfetter the son and should it be successful, a deadly blow will be dealt to artistic freedom in this country.

We trust that you may find it possible to give the fund your assistance. Subscriptions may be made payable to the treasurer, A. E. Malone, Thomond House, Rialto.

Thanking you in anticipation of your support,

Yours faithfully,
Hugh McCartan, Secretary
    Weldon Subscription Fund.
A.E. Malone, Treasurer [8]

While many important names in literature appeared as signatories, a few who might have been expected to support the appeal demurred. George Bernard Shaw was as ever practical:

> 10 Adelphi Terrace, with Bernard Shaw's compliments.
> I return these as they may be useful to you. The case does not seem to me to be one to make a public stand on. It is hard on Mr Weldon that his legal remedy has failed and it should have lain in the criminal, not in the civil courts. But I see no good in throwing good money after bad trying to get a jury to agree in a case of that nature.

G.B.S. [9]

Lord Justice O'Connor's address as reported in the press, together with his charge outlined by the Appeal Fund Secretary, suggest that a successful appeal was possible. Only a small sum was collected, however, far from enough to reopen the case. James Weldon's health declined rapidly from this point on but he remained obdurate.

Nor was Brinsley MacNamara giving up. On 16 January 1924 he called to the Board of Education demanding the return to his father's school of roll-books which had been taken for the trial and not given back. He also made a plea for the intervention of the Minister in the case, since the boycott was continuing, but was told that the Minister could not resolve the issue while the averages remained low. Brinsley then inquired whether his father could be allotted full pension if he retired immediately. Under the circumstances this would have seemed a sensible solution but pension rules were statutory, so the proposal was rejected. [10]

A new fact then emerged; in giving a fresh summary of the case, Education Board memoranda contended that after the book-burning and start of the boycott, a decision was taken in Delvin, by whom it is not clear, that Maunsel's should suspend further publication. This suggests that James Weldon may have been forced not only to repudiate *The Valley of the Squinting Windows*, but also to halt further production of the book. In any event, copies came in from the United States.

Minor harassment of the schoolteacher by Delvins continued and the Board of Education accused him of having been absent without notice from his school when an inspector called to collect roll-books and other registers for the trial. The Board adopted a convenient attitude to Brinsley's representations: they considered the case still to be *sub judice* and therefore not open for comment.

The Rev. Patrick Tuite died on 14 June 1924 at eighty-one years of age. During his ministry, since 24 April 1892, he had finished building the church at Killulagh and cleared its debt. Delvin church had been pointed and renovated, and he had acquired ground for a new cemetery. It is for his part in *The Valley of the Squinting Windows*, however, that he is most remembered.

The Rev. James Flynn succeeded him as parish priest and was appointed Vicar Forane. During his first sermon in Delvin he is said to have stated: 'I stand before you in fear and trepidation.' On 20 February 1925 he wrote to the Board of Education, referring to the Weldon case and stating that the teacher had tendered notice of his resignation to Mr McMahon, inspector, and was about to submit it to him as manager. The priest expressed his conviction that, with a good man as teacher, Ballinvalley Boys' School would be 'one of the biggest in the country outside the towns'. This Irish bull accompanied more facts on averages: there were still only twenty or twenty-one on the rolls and boys were travelling long distances to other schools. He assured the Board that he was 'not trying to work a job of any kind'.[11]

On 27 February James Weldon resigned. Some time thereafter he suffered a heart attack and was unconscious for four days. Meanwhile the Board pressed its opportunity to effect amalgamation.

> Fr Dwane was again faced with a grave difficulty. This particular school ... had given him an unfathomable amount of trouble ... He would have to be extra careful this time. The eyes of the parishioners were upon him ... So, having pondered the matter for weeks, he at length came to a wise plan. He would transfer his best schoolmaster, Michael Glynn.[12]

Fr Flynn was dogged. After arriving in Delvin he had announced from the altar that the children were illiterate leaving school. Ballinvalley was 'a flourishing school before Weldon' and would be one again. The priest succeeded in resisting amalgamation and Thomas Healy of Edenderry National School was appointed principal of Ballinvalley (Male) School. Within days of his taking up the position the number of pupils on the roll jumped to forty. On 10 June Fr Flynn proudly informed the Board that it had risen to forty-nine – then sought and obtained a Junior Assistant Mistress (JAM).

Flynn then went about rectifying the fact that Healy was receiving only a salary commensurate with the low averages of his predecessor, in spite of increasing attendances. The case was brought to the Minister for Finance, who agreed to regard it as exceptional. Healy was to get 'the salary which he would normally receive in a school with an average of from 30 to 40 pupils together with annual capitation grant at the rate of 10/= (less 10%) per pupil per annum on the actual average attendance of pupils between three and fifteen years of age'.

By 12 October Fr Flynn was pushing for a permanent assistant. His claim that the ordinary daily attendance was then 58 or 59 is not borne out by official figures. Nevertheless, the rapid progress must have been galling for James Weldon. He watched his old schoolhouse thrive from the teacher's residence he continued to occupy (as his predecessor had done). It is difficult to feel anything but pity for a man so wronged.

On 27 January 1926 an assistant mistress was appointed to Ballinvalley Boys' School. The boycott was over, the Valley had had its way. James Weldon, broken in health and spirit, moved to Avoca, Co. Wicklow in the spring of 1926.

> For what must have appeared long years to him, but which were in reality only a couple of seasons, he effected, not without a hard struggle, retirement from the life around him.[13]

AN APPEAL

WELDON SUBSCRIPTION FUND

Mr. James Weldon, a National School Teacher at Ballinvalley School. Delvin, Co. Westmeath, instituted an action against certain defendants resident in the village of Delvin, claiming damages for alleged conspiracy to boycott his school, as a result of which his salary and pension are seriously diminished. The reason for the alleged conspiracy was the publication of a book entitled "The Valley of the Squinting Windows" by his son, who writes under the nom-de-plume of "Brinsley McNamara." The trial of the action took place recently in Dublin and the jury disagreed. A new trial is therefore necessary in order to obtain a definite decision on the serious issues involved.

In view of Mr. Weldon's circumstances, and also of the fact that we regard the case as one affecting the entire community and the future of our social life, we appeal to the public for support.

Subscriptions should be sent to the Treasurer, A. E. MALONE, THOMOND HOUSE, RIALTO, DUBLIN.

SIGNED,

W. B. YEATS.
GEO. W. RUSSELL (Æ).
OLIVER ST. J. GOGARTY.
JAMES STEPHENS.
JAMES G. DOUGLAS.
AODH DE BLACAM.
EAMON O'DUIBHIR.

18th December, 1923.

SIX

THE BOOK

'A putrid book,' he could hear Phelim O'Brien say in 'The Daffodils,' while
the others showed their enjoyment of this opinion around the greasy tables,
a certain young man from the south hitting his knee continually as he
endorsed the opinion of his master – 'Like nothing so much as a bloody big
field, all weeds and thistles and dirt, where a fellow would want to go out with
a bloody big scythe and slash around him before the damn thing would be
even bearable to walk through.'[1]

When *The Valley of the Squinting Windows* was published, *The Irish
Times* did not have a weekend supplement giving generous space to
book reviews. Instead, there was a Saturday column largely devoted to
non-fiction about the Great War, with novels nudged into a few lines
at the end. On 8 June 1918 the following unsigned notice appeared:

This is a very disappointing novel for, though it has some local Irish colour,
the story and the characters appear to us to be truer pictures of life in
Manchester or Liverpool slums than in a remote Irish village. We hope
earnestly that the picture is false; we know that it is hideous and depressing
in the extreme. There is not a good man or a decent woman on the closely-
crowded canvas or one gay and happy scene in the book. Sordid from cover
to cover, it is a production which must vex every lover of Ireland, nor has it
even, in its tragic gloom, risen to those heights of sorrow which purify the
spirit through pity and fear. Its gloom is that of the public-houses and back-
lanes. There is no breath of the sorrow which inexorable fate brings and the
sternness of Nature accentuates. It is not a book which any Irishman can read
with honest pride, and we gladly close it and hope never to open it again.

The *Irish Independent* commended the reserve with which the author
brought the tragedy to its powerful climax; the reviewer admired
MacNamara's 'delightfully easy style' which '[added] considerably to
the reader's entertainment' and thought that, in the hands of a non-
Catholic, the plot 'would be made a hash of'. (Presumably
the *Irish Independent* critic felt that Mrs Brennan's obsessive desire to
have 'a priest in the family' could not have been presented with the

same passion by a non-Roman Catholic author.)

E.A.B. in *The Freeman's Journal* thought it 'an interesting and well written story, remarkably free from the weaknesses of most first novels, and wholly emancipated from the bonds which shackle so many works of Irish fiction'. The reviewer credited Brinsley MacNamara with having a real gift of story-telling, 'a discreet sense of the use of dialect and a perception of reality as unspoiled by convention as his style is free from affectations'. The *Birkenhead News* thought only *Jude the Obscure* could surpass *The Valley of the Squinting Windows* or George Douglas's *The House with the Green Shutters*, with which it had been compared. The review in *The New York Sun* stated: 'The story is as strong in its way as the Synge plays themselves and will haunt everyone who reads it as long as *Riders to the Sea*.' *The St Louis Mirror* considered it 'a work of art' while the *New York Globe* pronounced: 'Great novels, combining both dramatic interest and literary excellence, are not so common that anyone can afford to pass *The Valley of the Squinting Windows*.'

A decade later Andrew Malone described the book as the most realistic novel on Irish life of the previous ten years. It was, he said:

> merciless in its objectivity, the author having no thesis to defend nor cause to attack; and its analysis of the Irish rural mind is unmatched in the wide range of contemporary Irish literature ... Certainly Brinsley MacNamara's peasants are akin to the peasants of Maupassant and Chekov [*sic*] with both of whom he suggests interesting and profitable comparisons ... It was the gossip, and the temptations of the 'seven pubs' of Garradrimna, that brought John Brennan to the ruin which had enveloped his father. The malicious spite of a little village has rarely been so powerfully and so vividly presented in fiction ... The apparent peace of little villages is attractive to the dweller in big cities, but in this book the apparent peace of one little village, at least, is exposed in a way that would deter any seeker after seclusion and quiet from settling in its neighbourhood ... In his portrayal of Rebecca Kerr, the unsuspecting little schoolteacher, Mr Brinsley MacNamara is at his best. Charming, cultured, modern, she brings a refreshing breeze into the village. But in the end she too is overcome and stifled by the miasma of hatred that seems to be the only distinctive quality of the village.

On the basis of his first four novels, Malone declared MacNamara a 'writer of considerable achievement'.[2] A year on, in July 1929, his appreciation of the author appeared in *The Dublin Magazine*. Here he discussed an interesting aspect of *The Valley of the Squinting Windows*. The book, he said, was true sociologically and artistically:

Unerringly the novelist struck at the weakest point in the Irish rural social system: its treatment of women. Politically, women are free in Ireland, but in social life they are just the servants of men. So Mrs Brennan was sacrificed, as was Rebecca Kerr. *The Valley of the Squinting Windows* is the story of an entire village – but it is mainly the story of two much-wronged women.

Time modified this judgment and in a foreword to the 1964 Anvil edition of *Windows* Peadar O'Donnell wrote:

> He felt those were days when people might behave better if cut down to size. He had Ireland in mind, but he used his village as his blackboard. He was a man with a mission, a dangerous state of mind for an author.

In the same edition Benedict Kiely claimed:

> Brinsley did have in mind to startle people to take a sharper look at themselves. He had no time – and that's to put it mildly – for writers who encouraged the old, swaggering attitudes.

Adding, in a radio interview with Eavan Boland:

> There may still be a few people around who think what the young novelist did in 1918 [was] deliberately [to] draw the face of the village of Delvin with a leer and a squint and moles beyond number. As is fairly common knowledge the process isn't as simple as all that. The writer takes a bit here and a bit there, chops, changes, adds ... so that at times even people whose traits he was using as raw material might not in the end recognize themselves. On the other hand, some people over-identify.[3]

Boland discussed the Irish novelist's readership and his relationship with the community:

> [Brinsley MacNamara's] book is about the power of superstition and gossip ... and I think the people of Delvin recognized themselves just enough to feel it thoroughly insulting ... But why did it all happen? ... Why ... all that fuss? The answer probably lies back in the whole question not just of the relationship of the writer with the community but of his relationship with history ... *The Valley of the Squinting Windows* is ... a good book rather than a great one. What is great about it, though, is the enormous shift it represents in the emphasis and direction of the Irish writer. During the nineteenth century there was that whole constellation of novelists – Carleton, Lever, Lover – who had all written through the turbulent lifetime of Ireland in the nineteenth century, not to mention Lady Morgan. There was a common force binding all those writers. They lived in an occupied country and they wrote for the occupier ... Then suddenly that troubled century comes to an end and a great deal starts to happen. There's the Gaelic League and the new theatre and the

library associations and the local conspiracies and almost unwritten samizdats start circulating amongst the people ... The fact that it had been the British, not the Irish, who for more than a hundred years had been the clients of Irish writers meant that the Irish had no experience whatsoever of the upheavals and frictions and irritants that gradually built a rapport between the writer and his community ... They wanted support, consolation, the stuff of a new national self-image. History had offered them enough grief. They felt they had a right to look to their culture for something a bit different ... But there's something apart from just the friction that comes from the community seeing themselves in a book. There's ... one whole aspect of the relationship between ... Brinsley MacNamara and his book ... which is the most disturbing aspect of all ... The later struggle between writers and the community in Ireland really happened through the agency of the censorship laws. People like Kate O'Brien, Patrick Kavanagh and Ben Kiely, indeed, had their books banned because of a piece of legislation that had gone through the parliament and was on the books. That was bad enough ... But ... I think that the conflict that happened between the people of Delvin and Brinsley MacNamara illustrates what's worse. The most pernicious thing that can happen to a writer is that he lives in a community that practises censorship. The people of Delvin, with their hysterical and dogmatic response, were autonomously censoring what didn't flatter them; what didn't reassure them. They were excluding it from their consciousness in the most brutal and violent way. Their crude action stands with all the rough edge of hysteria – the burning, the meetings, the boycott, and I'm not sure that it isn't even more destructive than the official censorship ...

Here I think it's right to remove the whole issue from the village of Delvin and its people and see it in its right perspective. 'When a country has made a long fight for freedom,' said Brinsley MacNamara himself, 'there is a feeling, pardonable enough, that it is in a sense traitorous to delve too deeply into the frailties of one's own people.' And that's it in a nutshell. The uproar in Delvin was not alone, an isolated incident, it was part of a long, disturbing sequence of harassment of the writer which happened in this country in or around that time. The sustained campaign against John Synge was part of that. *The Playboy* scandalized the nationalists. And there were riots against O'Casey ... and it didn't stop there. [It continued] to get worse until you had that absurd spectacle ... of the police watching Patrick Kavanagh's flat to seize *The Great Hunger*. In a sense I think that is the worst of all – using the people's police against the people's poet ...[4]

To Eavan Boland's examples could be added Alan Simpson's imprisonment for staging *The Rose Tattoo* by Tennessee Williams at the Dublin International Theatre Festival in May 1957, and Salman Rushdie's *fatwa* or death sentence for *The Satanic Verses* pronounced in February 1989.

Mícheál Ó hAodha, a friend and colleague of the author, considers that, despite its melodrama, *The Valley of the Squinting Windows* is important to the development of the Irish novel:

> Although George Moore had learned realism from Zola, Brinsley MacNamara was the first to write a novel of rural Irish life from his own personal experience (Murray had done this on the stage and Daniel Corkery pre-dates him as a short-story writer). MacNamara was the forerunner of such writers as O'Flaherty and Peadar O'Donnell and so has a special place in any survey of Irish fiction.[5]

If some evaluations of MacNamara's best-known book were distorted by the furore it occasioned, in the main professional judgments were made. This became easier as the memory of the burning, the boycott and the court case faded. In 1963 Brinsley MacNamara died and in 1964 the first paperback edition of *The Valley of the Squinting Windows* appeared. Each event prompted recollections of Delvin and reappraisals. Brinsley's son, Oliver Weldon, writing in the *Irish Independent*, described how Maunsel's, the publishers, had just sent a few copies of the original printing to England for review when the trouble started in Delvin:

> Fearing they might be molested in Dublin, they withdrew the book for a time and made no further efforts to have it reviewed or sold in England. Its sale in Ireland proceeded later in a very timid way.[6]

Distinguished critics gave their frank assessments. T. C. Murray wrote that MacNamara gave us 'that cleansing of the spirit through pity and terror that is the virtue of all genuine tragedy'.[7] Peadar O'Donnell referred to him as

> one of the small band of Irish writers who elected to fight it out on the home scene [whose early works had an] exciting influence … on young writers who had made the village their world. He was a writer of very great stature, whose work will have its periods of revival far down the years. His reputation will creep up on the great names in Irish letters.[8]

Professor Thomas Flanagan of the University of California contributed a long review to the *Irish Press* on 18 July 1964. He recalled how Delvin people had always feared that Brinsley MacNamara would 'do the Playboy on them' and asserted that their response to the novel became 'internationally notorious'. Both claims seem exaggerated. Initially, the Delvins were quite pleased about their

village having a published author, and there is no evidence to suggest
that they feared what Brinsley would write. International notoriety is,
arguably, confined to Irish-American/Canadian literary circles and
older Irish emigrants. Sean McMahon, the Derry writer and critic,
agrees: 'It would be a gross exaggeration to say, à la Emerson, that
embattled farmers of Delvin fired shots heard around the world.'
Without the surrounding controversy the book might have gone
unnoticed, Flanagan speculated, remarking that it was known to
many only for its title and for the brouhaha it caused. It was now
possible to view it more dispassionately:

> the [book] takes its place in the literary tradition of the revolt from the village.
> It was a tradition which, in America, at roughly the same time produced ...
> *Winesburg, Ohio*, *The Spoon River Anthology*, *Main Street* and several lesser
> works ... Like his American contemporaries [MacNamara] has been hailed
> as the fore-runner of realism but again, like them, a strong hidden strain of
> romanticism runs through his work ... Speaking of his intentions Mac-
> Namara later wrote that the best service a writer 'can do his country is to raise
> its self respect by attempting to lift it out of the dark realm of sham and cant
> and humbug by holding up the mirror truthfully', and certainly the *Valley* is
> ruthless in its pursuit of cant and sham ... Every aspect of village life is held
> up to examination and few escape censure. The essential tragedy issues from
> the mean need for respectability which dominates the town with its double
> row of squinting windows ... The tragedy is enacted in an atmosphere of
> claustrophobic gossip, whispers, suspicion – an atmosphere in which all
> spontaneous ... feeling is chilled or foredoomed ...
>
> Garradrimna is no more an actual Irish village than *Wuthering Heights* is
> a sober report of life in Yorkshire. Rather it is a distillation of everything in
> Irish life which the author detested, heightened and distorted with romantic
> intensity. I am speaking of fictional credibility. The local fate which author
> and novel suffered does suggest, it must be admitted, that he drew it with scant
> exaggeration ... It is difficult to accept ... that he did not choose to go into
> conflict with his own village. This suggests an uncanny naivety on
> MacNamara's part. He must surely have known that his neighbours would
> be hurt, and hurt deeply, by the book which is, in fact, marred in places by the
> suspicion that a young man is paying off old debts. And when you're engaged
> in that sport you cannot expect to be elected mayor ... Like many good books
> it is written out of love and hate. Like many imperfect ones, it is written by a
> man who could not come to terms with his vision. He seems to have been
> puzzled by his persistence in loving that which he must hate so easily and this
> puzzlement finds its reflection in the novel. But this is also a quality which
> attracts us to the book. It implies the honesty of feeling that went into its
> creation.[9]

As Brinsley MacNamara began to find his place in Ireland's literary history, respect was mixed with reticence in recording worth. Michael McDonnell, who had submitted a thesis on the author to Trinity College, Dublin, contributed the entry for MacNamara to the 1980 *Dictionary of Irish Literature*.[10] He wrote:

> The dedicated novelist who worked arduously to produce four novels of high merit in less than six years was to produce only three more novels in the remaining forty years of his life – two of which, *The Various Lives of Marcus Igoe* (1929) and *Return to Ebontheever* (1930), were partially completed during this same six-year period ... After *The Glorious Uncertainty*'s financial success his future life was to be far more given to the life of literary raconteur and popular, fashionable dramatist than to the personally more demanding and less visible life of *enfant terrible* of Irish fiction.

McDonnell deemed *The Various Lives of Marcus Igoe* MacNamara's best novel: 'an intensely personal, self-evaluative, tragicomic fantasy ... worthy of a Flann O'Brien ... [it] must eventually be his most acclaimed work and the assurance of his real place in twentieth-century Irish literature',[11] an evaluation confirmed by Benedict Kiely:

> It is greatly to his credit that when he wrote [it] he was not misled by foolish praise of his supposed realism to attempt to play Zola to the life of an Irish cobbler. He followed the natural twist of genius and wrote his best book.[12]

Richard Fallis, Associate Professor of English at Syracuse University, New York, declared MacNamara

> a writer with some very serious flaws but, at his best, able to create a compelling vision of the meanness of rural Ireland ... *The Valley of the Squinting Windows* ... is a portrayal of the power of gossip in what is really an agricultural slum ... His feel for the midlands is real enough.[13]

Éire-Ireland, the Irish American Cultural Institute's journal of Irish studies, featured lengthy critiques of *The Valley of the Squinting Windows* in its Spring 1968 and Summer 1983 editions. Sean McMahon wrote in the earlier piece that 'The topographical details ... placed it firmly in Delvin and district'; he felt that events surrounding the burning 'lent a gaudiness to the book that clouded a true vision of it', claiming that it was neither MacNamara's 'best nor most characteristic work'. He went on:

> It is easy to see how it could be regarded as a slur on the fair name of Holy Ireland, especially when we consider the effect of the word *shift* in 1907, about

the time MacNamara had joined the Abbey company ... [It is] very much a novel of its time and, in its florid strength and slightly unctuous treatment of sex, full cousin to the best-sellers of the day. Though the castigation of the hypocrisy, the malevolence and the narrowness of the valley people is perfectly proper, it is done in such loving detail that the moral attitude of the author becomes questionable. The work lacks detachment and, in spite of an apparent sympathy, mercy ... though no more detached about life in the Irish Midlands than Scott Fitzgerald was about The Jazz Age, he is superb at conveying the nightmare of the choking, brutalizing life of the small farmer and the shop-assistant in small towns.

McMahon also noted that there was cheer as well as gloom in the villages and countryside:

His picture of the valley is blacker than black. The three million of us who do not live in Dublin, Belfast or Cork know that the average Irish small town is no Cranford. There is spite, viciousness and hate ... But there is love and joy in these places too. And MacNamara will not admit it.[14]

In her 1983 contribution, 'Brinsley MacNamara's Penny Dreadful', Ruth Fleischmann of the University of Bielefeld accused the author of throwing away the opportunity to show 'the stagnation, mental and material, in which the men of small property had become becalmed; to show the predatory relations within the family and between the sexes, the women being aggressors as well as victims; to show the price to be paid for attempting to better oneself at the cost of others'. Unsparingly pointing out major defects in the structure of the work, she suggests how they could have been avoided:

MacNamara fails to decide on any perspective. Instead, he lets himself be drawn without resistance towards all the pious and penny-dreadful stereotypes hovering over his material, and he flits from one to the other picking up bits of shoddy prefabricated clichés. These prevail over his original, sadly neglected material. In place of the sombre comedy of rural life we find a trashy tale of terror, tears, and tripe which the author has the audacity to present, at the end, as a tragedy ... The pattern discernible ... is that of masochistic exhibitionism alternating with sadistic fantasies, the former usually reserved for the women, and the latter for the men ... MacNamara, no doubt, intended his book as an attack on the Stage-Gael peasant. But attacks are not necessarily well conducted; nor does it always follow that what the assaulter offers as an alternative represents an advance. Delineating a face is a fine art, and MacNamara has not mastered it. His characters are all faceless, and to cover the nakedness he claps on another mask – not that of Paddy-the-Clown, nor of the suffering saint, but the mask of malignant depravity.

Fleischmann compared MacNamara unfavourably with Canon Sheehan and criticized those who placed him ahead of his time: 'With regard to his subject matter [he] is not ahead of but with his time.' The author was accused of letting a good idea dissolve into a general feeling of disgust:

> Instead of studying the object of his criticism, he is preoccupied with the spectacle of himself as the social critic and seer letting them have it … Because MacNamara's knowledge of rural Ireland is so insignificant, because of his incompetence as a writer, and because of the arrogant, spiteful, and inaccurate abuse which is the content of the novel, *The Valley of the Squinting Windows* cannot be recognized as a novel of social criticism or as a realistic novel.[15]

Contemporary histories of literature pay slight regard to MacNamara. Roger McHugh and Maurice Harmon, while noting that *Windows* had a *succès de scandale*, considered that 'Today it would be regarded as rather tame and not particularly well written.'[16] Seamus Deane, on the other hand, found it 'one of the most effective exposures of the narrow meanness of village life … In contrast, *The Various Lives of Marcus Igoe* … is a meditation on the autonomy of literature, elaborated in a fey and whimsical style.'[17]

An appraisal of MacNamara's work by Meath-born author Kevin Casey appeared in 1984, after the seventh paperback edition of *The Valley of the Squinting Windows*. Reviewing it with its successor *The Clanking of Chains*, Casey suggested that the year of publication was pertinent:

> If it had been published before the 1916 Rising, before there was a new and idealised sense of national identity, it is at least possible that it would have attracted much less hostility. It is interesting to note, however, that Brinsley MacNamara was unimpressed by revolutionary fervour and his second novel, *The Clanking of Chains*, published in 1920, is an early record of disillusionment. The contrast between national rhetoric and aspiration and the actual fabric of smalltown Irish life, could be said to be his essential theme. It is this contrast that *The Clanking of Chains* examines and that *The Valley of the Squinting Windows* provoked. By acting as they did, those inhabitants of Delvin who wanted to deny the veracity of the novel actually confirmed it [a theory offered by Lord Justice O'Connor]. It is not unusual for communities to resent the manner in which they are depicted by the artist, but it is not usual for life to imitate art with such ironic perfection.[18]

Casey found *The Valley* disappointingly dated, ponderous and oddly coy, proceeding without change of pace with an all-too-predictable logic: 'It is not the piece of naturalism that it has sometimes been described as, but rather a dramatised version of a certain reality … The book … has much of the character of a tract.' He found *The Clanking of Chains* in every way better and more interesting, and credits MacNamara with being 'one of the first writers to detect the existence of the Grocer's Republic, aware, less than four years after the selflessness of the Easter Rising, of the unremitting selfishness of Irish smalltown life'.

After seven decades of literary commentary, there are, just as in Delvin, pro-book and anti-book schools of thought. With over 67,000 paperback copies sold between 1964 and 1988 the title has gained an emblematic significance, and 'Remember *The Valley of the Squinting Windows*!' is a warning call to Irish authors, a reminder of the punishment that hypersensitive fellow countrymen can administer. As an admirer of MacNamara said, however, 'Whether [the academics] like it or not, it has become a classic.'

> He was thinking of all the torture he had been the means of causing … He would turn over a new leaf now … This was to be the end of his bitterness against Garradrimna. Sure maybe it wasn't Garradrimna at all, only himself.[19]

SEVEN

THE SEQUEL

the curve of his life should never again return to clay. Henceforth his life must be phrased in bronze.[1]

In December 1924 James Stephens, owing to failing health, offered his resignation to the National Gallery of Ireland, where he was Registrar. Early in 1925 Brinsley MacNamara was appointed in a temporary capacity. Stephens's resignation became effective in December of that year and MacNamara was made permanent; he remained as the last of the Gallery's independent registrars until 1960. Detractors claim that his 'political clout' secured the position. John Weldon used his pen-name on official correspondence and all Gallery business referred to him as Brinsley MacNamara. The appointment did not pay well and royalties brought in little income. Circumstances were difficult, therefore, and while he persisted with his novels, play-writing was essential for survival.

On 11 February 1926 Joseph Holloway referred to the protest at the Abbey Theatre against O'Casey's *The Plough and the Stars* and recorded hearing Dan Breen, the Tipperary revolutionary, say: 'Mrs Pearse, Mrs Tom Clarke, Mrs Sheehy-Skeffington and others were in the theatre to vindicate the manhood of 1916.' Holloway must have returned the following night for on 12 February he observed: 'A detective-lined theatre. No disturbance up to the end of Act II. I left for home ... I saw O'Casey, Brinsley MacNamara, Liam O'Flaherty ... and others of the dirt cult in a group in the vestibule.' Unfortunately, the man about stage doors heard no words but he remarked later that MacNamara did not like the play, thinking much of its dialogue involved and imitative.

James Weldon was now retired to Valleymount House, Avoca in Co. Wicklow, where he was well liked and sought out by visitors. Happy there, he suffered less from his heart condition, which it was always assumed had been brought about by the trauma of the boycott. About the time James Weldon was settling down in Wicklow an inspector was visiting his first school at Killough. An entry in the subsequent report reads ironically: '*Molaim leabhar a bhaineann le saol na tuaithe a fháil mar léightheoir.*' * [2]

While he visited his parents regularly, Brinsley MacNamara had settled into literary Dublin where he developed friendships and enmities with leading personalities of the day.

Despite Yeats's criticism of *Look at the Heffernans!*, the play became an outstanding box-office success at the Abbey. Michael McDonnell held that MacNamara 'compromised himself as an artist to produce commercially successful Abbey formula plays'.[3] (The love-hate relationship between the crowd-drawing playwright and the theatre Board of Directors was a foretaste of more recent times when John B. Keane was shunned by the National Theatre even as his work proved tremendously popular in the provinces. Eventually, when it was realized that by scratching any Dubliner's skin a countryman could be discovered, Keane's plays were introduced to the Abbey repertoire and made an impact that led to a feature film being made of *The Field*.)

MacNamara's play *The Master* was drafted as 'The Boycott' and its pattern is familiar. The action takes place in the Parochial House, school and teacher's residence of Clunnen, a village in the Irish midlands. James Quinn, an elderly, drinking schoolmaster, is sacked by the National Board; his replacement is boycotted and a mob attacks the school. F. J. McCormick, Arthur Shields and Maureen Delaney were in the cast when the play opened on 6 March 1928. Ballinvalley must have been in mind as its author lectured on the play during an INTO-sponsored evening at the Mullingar County Hall on 17 November 1928. The *Westmeath Examiner* report of the following week (24 November) quoted from his talk entitled 'The Author and his Characters':

> One should be patriotic, political and popular, write with one's tongue in one's cheek, and say of the Irishman anywhere, 'His vices are those of the stranger, while his virtues are peculiarly his own.' But because I am a native

---

* I recommend that a book concerned with the life of the countryside should be procured as a reader.

of this place and speak here in Mullingar, which was the scene of much of my early childhood … I must come at once at another aspect of the matter … what I have to say is in the nature of an explanation and other than any form of defence, the necessity for which, to my mind, does not arise. Whenever I come to the Midlands it is generally supposed that I am on the prowl for characters and that there is always the danger through meeting one, of finding oneself later as a character in a story or a play (laughter). Some flatter themselves that they have been immortalized through their martyrdom by me.

His father had had to defend himself from 'the creatures of his son's imagination' and MacNamara thought it a tribute to the power of this imagination that he created characters,

as a reviewer might say, of such real flesh and blood that they are nothing short of real, living people, but at the risk of demolishing this aspect of my reputation I will say here and now the attributing to me of this power is wholly extravagant and erroneous. It is largely a question of the imagination of my supposed characters against my imagination.

He concluded his lecture:

If I began to apologize for my writings I should have to go to too many places. It is said in other countries of *The Valley of the Squinting Windows* that it is no more an attack upon Ireland, than it is upon Corsica or Madagascar or any part of those distant islands. It is merely a study of the tragic results of envenomed gossip in a small community.

This was a courageous speech to make in a town so near Delvin and so soon after his father's court case. The Chairman of Westmeath National Teachers' Organization, John Casey of Milltown, proposed the vote of thanks by likening MacNamara to Thespis and proclaiming him a great builder and architect; he was also, like Synge, Yeats and Murray, one of the fathers of Irish drama. Describing the author as having torn aside 'the veil of Idealism and Phariseeism and painted us with our virtues, defects and vices', Casey went on: 'If our faults and weaknesses are held up occasionally to the public gaze, it is to raise a higher tone of culture and good breeding into society.'

In 1929 Brinsley MacNamara's most acclaimed novel, *The Various Lives of Marcus Igoe*, dedicated to his mother, was published in London by Sampson Low, Marston & Co. Also in that year Mandrake Press, London published *The Smiling Faces*, a collection of short stories.

Return to Ebontheever (Jonathan Cape, London) appeared in 1930 and in 1932 Brinsley MacNamara became one of the first members of the Irish Academy of Letters. His best-known tragedy, *Margaret Gillan*, received its first production at the Abbey on 17 January 1933 and was published the following year by George Allen & Unwin.

Between these two events, James Weldon died. His remains were returned to Walshestown, the cemetery for his old home at Hanstown, Ballinea. A tombstone there bears the inscription: 'In Loving Memory of James Weldon, Ballinvalley N.S., Delvin. Died 23 May 1933.'

Brinsley MacNamara had dedicated *The Valley of the Squinting Windows* 'TO ONE WHO WAITED FOR THIS STORY'. He was less reticent with *Margaret Gillan*: 'TO THE MEMORY OF MY FATHER.'

> MASTER: Their voices raised in anger to the last ...
>
> *Margaret Gillan* (Act 3 Finale)

During this period, MacNamara enjoyed the close friendship of Robert Maire Smyllie, famous editor of *The Irish Times*, and the Mayo-born poet F. R. Higgins. He was an affable companion at times to Patrick Kavanagh and Frank O'Connor (Michael O'Donovan) but relations became strained with both O'Connor and Austin Clarke (to whose wife, Lia, *née* Cummins, he had once been engaged) after a brawl they had with Higgins. The author was a popular member of the Dublin coterie of airmen, journalists, businessmen and assorted 'characters' who assembled in the Pearl Bar or in 'Indignation House' (the name given to Fannings, Lincoln Place because of its proprietor's roars of protest whenever the name Eamon de Valera was mentioned).

These were the times of the celebrated 'Boyne Walks'. Smyllie, Higgins and MacNamara, perhaps with another invited guest, would take the early-morning bus to Navan. After breakfast in Crinnion's Hotel the trio took the tow-path by the Boyne river to the bridge at Beauparc rocks and a winding road to Slane. Lunch in the village was followed by a further walk to Oldbridge and on to Drogheda.

In his poem entitled 'The Boyne Walk', dedicated to Smyllie, Higgins described MacNamara (erroneously referring to him as a Meath man):

> Heat trembled in halos on grass and on cattle
> And each rock blazed like a drunken face;

So I cried to the man of the speedy wattle
'In the name of Lot's wife will you wait a space?
For Adam's red apple hops dry in my throttle,'
And yet instead of easing the pace,
I saw on the broad blackboard of his back
His muscles made signs of a far greater chase,
Until as I tried to keep up on his track
Each pore of my skin became a hot spring
And every bone swam in a blister of pains
While all my bent body seemed as an old crane's
Lost in a great overcoat of wings.[4]

* * *

In Abbey Theatre minutes dated 17 April 1935 the name 'Brinsley MacNamara' is pencilled in among the list of directors. It appears in bold print on programmes up to and including Monday 16 September. Other directors were W. B. Yeats, Walter Starkie, Lennox Robinson, Dr Richard Hayes, Ernest Blythe and F. R. Higgins.

Public controversy had followed the 1928 rejection by the Abbey of O'Casey's expressionist *The Silver Tassie*. Private comment between directors and playwright had reached the national newspapers and soon the world press was reporting on further exchanges between Yeats and O'Casey.* For a while the rejection robbed the Abbey 'of a playwright who might have weaned its audience of [*sic*] the deadly diet of popular comedy and spurious realism'[5] unwittingly provided by MacNamara and others. The row was resolved in 1935 and the play opened on Monday 12 August with Barry Fitzgerald, M. J. Dolan, May Craig, Eileen Crowe and F. J. McCormick among the cast. Resolutions at meetings of Catholic and nationalist societies followed. Galway CYMS condemned 'violently the dramatic work of the Abbey Theatre in so far as it injure[d] the nation's prestige at home and abroad'.[6] Catholic periodicals called for a ban on O'Casey and for Yeats's dismissal; the President of *Conradh na Gaeilge* (The Gaelic League) wanted the theatre itself abolished. Then who should join the

---

* Yeats commented in his manuscript-book: 'Mr Shaw's and Mr Augustus John's admiration suggest that it was at least better than we thought it, and yet I am certain that if any of our other dramatists sent us a similar play we would reject it' (Joseph Hone, *W. B. Yeats, 1865-1939* [London 1942], p. 389).

ranks of the protesters but the man who had been subjected to similar abuse in Delvin – Brinsley MacNamara!

A statement of his appeared in the press claiming that he was never in favour of a production but as the only Roman Catholic member of the Board present when the work was accepted had felt powerless to prevent it. He had sought excisions from, and amendments to, the script:

> particularly with regard to the travesty of the Sacred Office in the second act … Not only had nothing been done to reduce the offensive quality … but it was more brazenly offensive than when I had seen its London production in 1929 … I warned the secretary of the theatre, Mr Eric Gorman, just as the rehearsals were beginning that, as the only Catholic director available at the moment, I urgently desired [certain changes] and asked him to acquaint the producer, Arthur Shields, of my wishes on the matter.[7]

Then MacNamara launched into a savage attack upon O'Casey, for whose 'vulgar and worthless plays' Abbey audiences had, he alleged, 'almost insane admiration'. The Abbey company was also berated for 'being borne wildly upon this wave of spurious Dublin popularity' and for its 'reverence for his work that has not been given to any other author who has ever written for the theatre'.

On 4 September another statement appeared in the *Irish Independent*:

> I cannot any longer remain a member of a Board whose directors have such an inadequate conception of their duty when faced with a serious situation and so I have sent in my resignation.

Obviously leaving himself open to a charge of jealousy, Brinsley is stoutly defended by Benedict Kiely:

> He might have disliked O'Casey and I could see why the two of them wouldn't get on … I never met O'Casey, but [he] could do the oddest things, you know. He was a very temperamental type … When Gabriel Fallon referred to him in the *Standard* as 'my friend Sean O'Casey' because of the old days [they spent] in the Abbey … well, O'Casey came up with a diatribe of a letter that he was no friend of his … this kind of thing … If you had a temperament like that I couldn't see you getting on too well with Brinsley, because he would stop you pretty short … From listening to Brinsley's conversation, I don't think he had any literary jealousy in him at all; I think he was above that. He was a very proud man.[8]

Some claim in his defence that Brinsley was objecting mainly to the vulgar methods of production employed by the Abbey. Micheál Ó hAodha disagrees:

> About the 'Tassie' and his obvious dislike for O'Casey, I think that Brinsley was one of the Dublin literary circle who resented O'Casey's great success in the twenties. Cf. Liam O'Flaherty, A.E., Austin Clarke, (probably Gogarty), Mrs Hannah Sheehy-Skeffington – all these people are on record, like Brinsley, in their begrudging attitude towards O'Casey … Some of Brinsley's attitude … stemmed from his dislike of Larkinism and the socialist theory of revolutionary activity.[9]

But the affair was best summed up in 1984 by Kevin Casey:

> One strange fact about Brinsley MacNamara remains to engage one's attention. From the tone of these two novels [*The Valley of the Squinting Windows* and *The Clanking of Chains*] and from the public reception accorded to the first, it might be expected that the author would stand on the side of artistic freedom; yet … he did his best to prevent a production of *The Silver Tassie* and wrote a pious letter to *The Irish Times*, explaining why he felt that 'certain portions of the play would be wantonly offensive to the largest section of our audience and to the country from which the Theatre derives its subsidy'.
>
> They must have had a good laugh at that in Delvin.[10]

After the Abbey production of *The Grand House in the City* in February 1936 Brinsley MacNamara's output diminished. His wife and son moved to Dublin that year and the three lived at 47 Waterloo Road. But the life of an author-raconteur and of Dublin's public-house literary bohemia was hard to reconcile with the gentler ways of Co. Clare, and the marriage was not without difficulties. Frances Weldon, Brinsley's mother, died in 1939 and was buried next to her husband in Walshestown. In that year too, MacNamara succeeded his friend Andrew Malone (Laurence Byrne) as drama critic of *The Irish Times*, a position he held until 1945. His own return to the Abbey with *The Three Thimbles* on 24 November 1941 – which those closest to him advised him to relegate to the back of the fire – was a chastening experience, relieved only when his novel *Return to Ebontheever* was reissued as *Othello's Daughter* in 1942. Two of his plays were translated into Irish in 1944: *The Glorious Uncertainty* (Mícheál Ó Siochfhradha's *An Tnúth Cráidhte*) and *Look at the Heffernans!* (Mícheál Ó dAndún's *Dearc ar na hIfearnánaigh!*).

*Marks and Mabel** was produced at the Abbey on 6 August 1945 and published the same year by James Duffy & Co. In the same year Talbot Press published another collection of short stories, *Some Curious People*, an appropriate title because of MacNamara's habit of prefacing a story or statement with 'Curious thing, you know!' Benedict Kiely re-enacts the philosophical meandering:

> A curious thing, you know! Your average Dublin working man, he goes into a public house and he drinks a pint, two pints, ten pints, nineteen pints! Boisterous, he curses, swears, sings songs, staggers home singing and sleeps it off.
>
>   But down where I come from – a curious thing, you know – life is different. The rivers flow smoothly, the grass grows high; the cattle graze quietly and peacefully. Your average working man lives in a cottage with his maiden aunt and cycles, perhaps, into Delvin and drinks a pint, drinks ten pints, nineteen pints – quietly. Cycles – quietly – home and murders his maiden aunt with a hatchet – curious thing, you know![11]

A row with R. M. Smyllie caused his departure from *The Irish Times*. The editor had published a letter from Hilton Edwards criticizing the terms of MacNamara's review of *The Skin of Our Teeth*, by Thornton Wilder, a Gate Theatre production by Edwards:

> Up to then Brinsley had been a constant attendant at the Smyllie salon in the back of the Palace Bar where literary Dublin foregathered round the Johnsonian figure ... and to which visiting literary men were drawn like pins to a magnet. After these sessions, the delicious MacNamara *mots*, drawled out between his teeth and well seasoned with wit and humour, circulated around Dublin like sputniks, losing nothing in their telling ... In later years the Palace lost its literary circle, the Pearl never quite achieved the same fame but Brinsley's cronies, when they wanted a bit of spice to their conversation, [repaired to a] pub at the top of Westland Row where many a young apprentice writer got his baptism of fire from the old master.[12]

MacNamara began to show more frequent signs of testiness brought on by a multitude of troubles, including a worsening arthritic condition. Drinking more heavily, he now made Kennedy's bar in Westland Row his retreat. While he offered a sympathetic ear to his young admirers, he found little solace himself.

---

*Tomás MacAnna regarded this as one of MacNamara's two best plays (the other being *The Glorious Uncertainty*).

All critics have written from incomplete knowledge of or background to Brinsley MacNamara. He suffered from the O'Casey clique – a small industry in itself, from the University College Dublin Roger McHugh tribe and from the world of academics in general.[13]

MacNamara still loved the countryside, and cared about Delvin but went back there only rarely to visit selected friends. Like Doalty Gallagher in Patrick McGill's *Glenmornan* and Sir J. M. Barrie, who hadn't dared appear in his native Kirriemuir after his 'Thrumms' series, MacNamara felt the occasional chill of isolation:

> They were still smiling, but already beginning to feel the emptiness of their hearts as they turned away. They would have to meet that man on the way out. They must look him in the face as proud as ever. But he was coming towards them.[14]

On 14 September 1948 MacNamara's son Oliver married Mary Coffey from Dundalk. The author would have called it a 'curious thing' that her father was friendly with Joseph Clyne of Delvin through their common interest in greyhounds. (Clyne is commemorated by the Joseph Clyne Memorial Cup trophy for the Midland St Leger at Mullingar greyhound track.)

A list of works performed at the National Theatre, *Abbey Plays 1899-1948*, was published in 1949 by Colm O'Lochlainn of At the Sign of the Three Candles, Dublin. A publisher's preamble to the volume noted that MacNamara modestly omitted his own work, which was 'notable … in quality and variety … [He] created a genre of light comedy all his own and distinctly and racily Irish.'

In 1951 H. R. Carter of Belfast published MacNamara's novella, *The Whole Story of the X.Y.Z.* During July of that year, he trod the rubble of the burnt-out Abbey Theatre with Benedict Kiely. *Look at the Heffernans!* was revived in 1952, and *Mairéad Gillan*, Brian Ó Nualláin's translation of *Margaret Gillan*, appeared in 1953.

During Brinsley MacNamara's last years, he did some work for Radio Éireann. *Mairéad Gillan* was broadcast and many of his other works adapted for radio. Mícheál Ó hAodha thought him a very good play-reader, for both the station and the Abbey. He recalled a day at Navan when Martin Maloney, champion jockey, rode five winners:

> That day, Brinsley, who never gambled much, kept out the winter chill by spending most of the time in the bar with Liam O'Flaherty. They were a

centre of attraction to all the County Meath crowd – until O'Flaherty started a row by calling some publican's beautifully dressed wife a 'Mullingar Heifer'. Brinsley was profuse in his apologies. He was always gentlemanly and courteous. He could be testy and sarcastic but he never used bad language.[15]

He also took part in a Radio Éireann series of portraits of Irish literary figures, including James Stephens and his friend F. R. Higgins, and was the star of some of the broadcasts. Seán Mac Réamoinn, who joined Radio Éireann in 1947 and worked with Brinsley, summed him up thus: 'A large man, he could be cranky; amiable, he loved talking about Westmeath and had no chip on his shoulder about Delvin.' He remarked on the author's humour and turn of phrase, recalling his description of a well-known slanderer as having made 'disinterested malice an art-form'. Seán, too, had a story:

> For one period, Brinsley chose to avoid Philip Rooney's company because he wasn't pleased with one of his adaptations. One day the pair met in a bar and Brinsley growled a greeting. Neither wishing to offend, drink followed drink but there was little conversation. Eventually Philip launched into a long-winded story. Only when he was reaching its end did he realize that the yarn was one he had heard a few days previously and its punch-line was at Brinsley's expense.
>
> Philip couldn't stop so he ended with some hurried nonsense, said goodbye and left. Micheál Ó hAodha told Philip some time later that he had been speaking to MacNamara who had said: 'Micheál, it's so sad about Philip. The other day he was blind drunk at ten o'clock and told the most silly long story that had neither rhyme nor reason.'[16]

MacNamara made a series of broadcasts called 'Conversations in Henry Street' with Professor Thomas Bodkin, Director of the National Gallery from 1939 to 1945 and Ambassador to Britain. One subject was his sometime adversary, Joseph Holloway, and Brinsley gave an entertaining account of a visit to the man who 'felt he had to be anywhere in which the word "Theatre" was mentioned'. A vast accumulation of papers, records and bric-à-brac was strewn about the floor and the only semblance of tidiness was in some pages of script, Holloway's review of a play just seen.

P. J. Bourke published *The Glorious Uncertainty* in 1957 and three years later, on 31 May 1960, crippled with arthritis, Brinsley MacNamara resigned from the National Gallery position.

One day thereafter his son Oliver accompanied him to Delvin and they stopped at Barry's public house (Harry Barry's mother had been identified with Mrs Wyse in *The Valley of the Squinting Windows*). After the long journey, Brinsley was barely able to stand and Oliver helped him from the car. Barry's was the bar previously owned by Joseph Clyne, who still ran the butcher's shop alongside. As the big but frail author was assisted towards the premises, Clyne stood at his shop doorway in a striped, bloody apron, a cleaver hanging from his belt, coldly staring at his old and crippled arch-enemy with no sign of recognition nor softening of features.

Brinsley MacNamara died intestate in St Patrick Dun's Hospital, Dublin at 2 a.m. on 4 February 1963, an embittered, isolated man. Preferring late-nineteenth-century realism to the Celtic Twilight, he had come to shun and be shunned by the literary establishment. At his funeral, Brian O'Nolan and Patrick Kavanagh both stood aside. Probate was granted to his son on 17 July. The prolific writer's worldly assets amounted to £688.

In the same year, Ballinvalley ceased to function as a national school.

> At last he fell somewhere in the soft, dewy grass. For a long while he remained
> here – until he began to realize that his vision was passing with the decline
> within him of the flame by which it had been created.[17]

DELVIN AREA

To Collinstown

MABES-TOWN

School and house.

To KILLUA

MULLAGH CRÓY

BALLINVALLEY

DUNGANS-TOWN

BALLYNA-SKEAGH

ELLENS-TOWN

MITCHELSTOWN

KILADDUGHRAN

DELVIN

MOORETOWN

C L O N Y N

CASTLE-TOWN

SOUTH HILL

DELVIN

JOHNSTOWN

BILLISTOWN

DRY-DERS-TOWN

CLADDAGH

DYSART

KILL-ÛLAGH

MULCHANS-TOWN

MARTINS-TOWN

WILLIAMSTOWN

HISKINSTOWN

MARTINSTOWN CROSS.

To Mullingar

N

School.

W — E

KILLOUGH

S

EIGHT

THE 'VALLEY'

Everyone has some one place in his life from which he never gets away, no matter how far he may appear to wander from it. I have been particularly fortunate in the place that was given me to stay in like that. It is the lovely Midland country where I was born and where all my young years were spent. I have been shown hills and the sea, and I have known some far cities; I have lived the greater part of my life in Dublin, but I have never ceased, even in the way I talk, to be a Midland man. My mind keeps going back there always, and it is there that I would wish to end my days.[1]

In *Ancient Westmeath*[2] Paul Walsh writes that the barony of Delvin was named after an ancient people collectively designated Delbna, who were of Munster origin and closely related to the *Dal gCais* or Dalcassians. Of four Delvins, three were in the Meath area and Delvin Mór, the Great Delvin, passed into Norman hands through a grant by Hugh de Lacy to Gilbert Nugent.

Westmeath has a history of localized strife and land agitation. Within Delvin parish in 1653 there were twenty-four confiscations and awards. During the year 1869 Co. Westmeath contributed half of all the crime committed in Leinster.[3] After the collapse of Fenianism in the wake of the unsuccessful rebellion of 1867, 'Ribbonism manifested great activity in Westmeath, Longford and adjacent counties in fighting the old Whiteboy cause against landlordism.'[4] In 1870 there were four murders. One farmer was shot for taking five acres off another and one died in a drunken brawl over land. The other victims were a steward and a process-server.

Beyond the low hills which rose out of the valley on its southern side, they ran along the twisty roads that led over flat country.[5]

At the outbreak of the Great War, Delvin was described in *MacDonald's Directory* as a parish of 18,278 acres with a population of 1737, although only 150 lived in the village itself. It was in Castlepollard RIC district and the *Westmeath Guardian* and *Westmeath Examiner* were its local newspapers. By the time Brinsley MacNamara's book appeared, the area bore witness to an unsettled past converging with a revolutionary present. A parody of Charles Kickham's poem 'Rory of the Hill' was still recited locally in praise of the unconvicted killer of Howard Fetherston, landlord of Bracklyn, who had been murdered in 1868; he was returning from Dublin with writs for eviction of tenants and as his carriage slowed down for the Hill of Knocksheban, he was shot dead.

> Fetherston said he'd raise the rent
> And turn out quite a few;
> But Rory, he stepped forward
> And says 'That will never do.'
> The landlord said he would not stop
> But the poorhouse he would fill
> 'Then, by George, I'll change your tune,'
> Said Rory of the Hill.

Tom Kelly, last of the Delvin Fenians, was remembered for his participation in the 1867 Rising and for returning from Australia to join in later agitations. Lord Greville's death after a family quarrel on the evening of his wife's funeral in January 1883, the Land League and the Barbavilla murder were discussed in hostelries over creamy pints. The courage and charisma of local representative Larry Ginnell and the exploits of his followers in the cattle-drives were relished.

'Lawrence of Arabia', T.E. Lawrence, had led the Arabs against the Turks during the Great War and Delvins enjoyed the story of his origins. His father, Robert Tighe Chapman (1846-1919), was of a line that built the eighteenth-century Killua Castle outside Clonmellon nearby. Chapman lived at South Hill, Delvin, where he had five daughters by his lawful wife. Born in 1888, T.E. was the second of five sons by the family governess, Sarah Junner (or Madden). Chapman had brought her from Scotland to South Hill, where T.E. was conceived, and eloped with her to England, where he was born. The name 'Lawrence' was assumed privately, though Lawrence was to remain conscious of his Irish origins and was proud at being invited to join the Irish Academy of Letters shortly before his untimely death in 1935.

The strong influence of the religious often threw its shadow over the area. In 1751 the vicar of Delvin, Rev. Moore Booker, was chastised by his bishop for encouraging the Methodist movement. In defence he cited increases in his congregation and in the number of communicants at his services. These included 'six Papists … [and] it was not a little affecting to see the poor creatures open their mouths for the bread to be put into them, as they had been used'.[6] He warned that Delvin might become like Athboy, 'a town full of Papists' where the cry 'a swaddler' was raised by the local 'Papist mob' who attacked one of his parishioners, Alexander Irwin, then 'knocked him down and beat him in a most cruel manner'.[7]

In 1780 the Roman Catholic Bishop of Meath, Dr Plunkett, visited Delvin and noted that 'the people were in general unacquainted with respect due to the house of God; for they spoke and were otherwise very dissipated during Mass'.[8]

Cock-fighting has always been popular in Delvin and a bar there, The Blue Hackle (previously called The Valley), proudly displays on its wall a large photograph of a fight in progress. Cock-fighting, illegal gambling, after-hours drinking and other pursuits just outside the law were often the subjects for satire in revues staged at St Patrick's Hall during the late seventies. The community seemed prepared to laugh at its own indiscretions. Why, then, was there such a hubbub about *The Valley of the Squinting Windows* ?

Theories abound concerning Brinsley MacNamara's inspiration for the title of his book, which was to become a byword for introvert parochialism in Ireland and elsewhere. An unusual interpretation comes from a schoolteacher who taught in Ballinvalley; the schoolroom had old-fashioned windows, with panes that looked like the bottoms of bottles. So when Brinsley was writing his book he would have to squint through these if he wished to look out – perhaps to see if Nellie was coming with the tea or if his father was on the prowl! Another theory links the title to Delvin's post office of the time, which was in a central building on the east side of the street. The busybody postmistress of the novel, if placed in real life, could survey the complete village of Delvin from the bay window in its parlour. If the window was draped in a lace curtain she could observe all, while remaining undetected. Still extant and called 'the squinting window' by some, it has a strong claim to perpetuity as the source.

A few steps from Ballinvalley School on the Castlepollard road stands the house of the Roper family. In MacNamara's time Anne

Roper was a dressmaker and, like the book's Mrs Brennan, worked from her back room. She had a son, Richard, who was studying for the priesthood but decided to opt out of clerical life. Mrs Brennan's son did the same. No city commentator or academic can assess the pain suffered by Anne Roper as a result of *The Valley of the Squinting Windows*, because having a priest in the family was a commonly cherished wish. The priest and the schoolteacher were looked up to in every locality; arbitrators, educators, advisers, disciplinarians, peace commissioners – they provided free extracurricular services to the community. Their repayment was respect – even if in some cases it was tendered through fear alone. The priest inspired a certain additional awe: a hand that struck one would wither, it was thought. Delvins told the story of the Sinn Féin priest, Fr Michael O' Flanagan, who came to the village for a rally (*c.* 1917) and was met by a torchlight procession. Lamps were placed in all but one window to honour his arrival. When villagers apologized for this exception, the priest warned that there would be plenty of light there soon. And there was; a fire broke out and the premises were burned to the ground. Given this atmosphere, a clerical student discovering he had no vocation was obliged to do one of two things: take Holy Orders, thereby submitting himself to a lifetime of faithless ministry, or – if he possessed the extreme courage – leave and become a 'spoiled priest'. His 'shame' was less than the family's for often he could emigrate.

Brinsley MacNamara was aware of this and must have known that Mrs Brennan's mien and occupation would provoke fury among the Ropers' friends and no little pleasure among their enemies.

As Delvins read on, their suspicion that Brinsley MacNamara pointed an unwavering finger at them was confirmed.

> This writing now, you know, at all at all? It's a great pity for a man of your scholastic attainments. As sure as day, there'll be trouble for me again about the school if you persist in it. Sure it stands to reason. This place is in the very middle of Ireland, and the people of Ireland simply don't like the Irish people to write … Books by people of other countries yes – and most pernicious stuff they are, invariably – but not books by their own.[9]

As soon as one local was 'spotted', the game was on to discover the remainder. There was Marse Prendergast, 'a superannuated shuiler and a terror in the valley,'[10] putting the fear of God into Mrs Brennan because of a dark secret she held. Delvin people speculated at length about the implications of this, airing the story of the illegitimate infant, child of a priest and his housekeeper. Wasn't it buried in Booker's Lake, right where the book's drowning took place? Would Marse be Margaret McKeon?

'Wasn't Séimí Growney, who called Joe Clyne the "Dreoilín" because of his big belly, out fishing there one day and didn't Fr Tuite come along and bid him the time of day: "Are you catching anything, Séimí?" said the priest. "Begad you'd never know what you might catch in this lake," whipped back Séimí, with a leer.'[11] Séimí, everyone reckoned, became Shamesy Golliher in MacNamara's book.

Garradrimna's Charlie Clarke bought the village's only car out of interests in bazaars and charities. If that were written today Patrick Murray, owner of Delvin's hackney-car then, would almost certainly win a libel case. Lord Greville became the Hon. Reginald Moore, and the wealthy landowning Shannons of the book were inspired by the Hegartys of Ballinskeagh, according to inhabitants of that townsland (then they add that the Valley's high and mighty Houlihans of Clonabroney might also have reflected the Hegartys, weakening their case).

The novel's Mrs Brennan knew of priests and relatives of priests who had grown rich; the Delvins probably did too, but it was prudent to profess horror at such an anti-clerical statement. Garradrimna's Padna Padna, whose affinities were somewhat pagan, was eighty years of age, got drunk every day and never went to Mass. Yet he was 'a striking figure as he moved abroad in the disguise of a cleric not altogether devoted to the service of God. He always dressed in a solemn black, and his coat was longer than that of a civilian.'[12] Some Delvin people thought that their local 'character' Patrick Devereaux was barely concealed in the description. Others, however, vowed James Mullen was the inspiration.

A story is told around Delvin of a man like Padna Padna. Tom was committed to Mullingar Mental Hospital, his most obvious symptom of illness being a belief that he was God Almighty. It was the custom for the hospital to have dances, to which friends of the staff were invited with the stipulation that they must dance with patients if requested. Biddy was invited to the floor by Tom, alias God Almighty.

Knowing about his imagined divinity she asked, 'When I die will I go to heaven?' With a look of disdain her partner replied: 'I never discuss business when I'm dancing.'

Every town had its Padna Padna. Dublin had Bang-Bang; Galway had a similar gunman; an urban district not far from Delvin had a young lad who behaved like a lorry – stopping, starting, even reversing along the footpath to the accompaniment of suitable sounds. Bartle Donohue, barber; Tommy Williams, gombeen man; Larry Cully, loafer: there is no shortage of similar individuals in Delvin – or in any other Irish village.

Had Delvin 'seven sleek publicans'? The Smiths had two premises, and there was Corcoran's, as The Midland Arms was most often called, the Esperanto Hotel, Fitzsimons' (now Gaffney's) and Clyne's. It is assumed that in 1918 there was a pub where O'Shaughnessy's is now, but in any event Delvin surely had a shebeen – like any self-respecting town!

Garradrimna's farmer parishioners looked after Fr Louis O'Keeffe's interests in cattle: grazing, buying, selling and lodging monies to his private account. This insult was compounded by having the priest renege at cards! At 'Twenty-Five' or 'A Hundred and Ten', the practice of withholding the playing of a trump was as despicable an act as ill-slipping a hound at a course or roughing the spurs of a bantam. But surely there can only have been amusement on reading:

> Yet it must not be thought that Father O'Keeffe neglected the ladies. In evenings in the village he might be seen standing outside the worn drapery counters back-biting between grins and giggles with the women of the shops. This curious way of spending the time had once led an irreverent American to describe him as 'the flirtatious shop-boy of Garradrimna'.[13]

Fr Tuite was then seventy-six years of age!

Because of Brinsley's friendship with Delvin's postman – already noted – Farrell McGuinness, Garradrimna's postman, is a likeable rogue who does little more harm than 'rising' those he meets on his rounds, especially Mrs Brennan.

The postmistress in Delvin at the time was Mary Cully (the wife of the postmaster, to be more precise). Her anger on reading the celebrated page forty-eight of *Windows* (pp. 42-3 in more recent paperback editions) can be imagined.

The gentle, refined Christina Barry lived with her mother at Mooretown and travelled with her each morning to Ballinvalley where she taught downstairs in the girls' school. Mrs Wyse, 'a woman who divided her energies between the education of other women's children and the production of children of her own ... passing down the street with her ass-load of children ... like a hen with her brood', was one of the villainesses of the Valley. Yet one of her alleged 'brood', Christina, smiles and says* it was wrong to treat James Weldon as the Delvin people did. Her late mother must have felt differently, for Christina's nephew adds that Rose Anne Barry's book and not Mrs Clyne's was the first to be burned.

Brinsley MacNamara's wife, formerly Ellen Degidon, denied that she was the Rebecca Kerr of the novel although like the book's heroine she had lodgings in the local RIC sergeant's house. Indeed the turnover of assistant teachers in Ballinvalley in the early years of the century bears out the statement in the novel: 'A new schoolmistress, well, well! Didn't they change them shocking often in Tullahanogue?'[14]

Mrs McGoldrick calling her children fancy names; Mickeen Connellan, the auctioneer who didn't pay as well as circus folk; Harry Holton, the comic disciple of Harry Lauder; the glutton of the Valley – sometimes there were contenders for association with minor characters. If all those examples were not enough to convince that Garradrimna was Delvin and its people Delvins through and through, there were the drama class rehearsals near the castle of the de Lacy's and the audience at the performance itself:

> The seven publicans of Garradrimna were there ... The Clerk of the Union continually adjusting and readjusting his lemon-coloured gloves. The old bespectacled maid from the Post Office sitting near the grey, bullet-headed postmaster, whose apoplectic jowl was shining.[15]

The schoolmaster of Garradrimna was the only one to escape unscathed. Master Donnellan was 'misunderstood', a 'quiet old man who didn't prate or meddle'.

In writing the novel Brinsley MacNamara can be held to have been either naïve – if he believed it would not cause a furore – or vindictive

---

* Christina Barry is now deceased.

– if the suggestion that he brought its publication forward is true. His use of neighbours' characteristics as copy in the novel is, however, legitimate. As the author explained to James Holloway, any novelist bases his characters on composites, departing from the known to the unknown. Chekhov read newspapers and used their reports of actual incidents in his works. Oscar Wilde portrayed the fops he met in the English salons, and James Joyce's 'stately, plump Buck Mulligan'[16] was his friend Oliver St John Gogarty. Patrick MacGill used the personalities of his native Donegal or the trenches of the Great War, while Synge was adept at finding Wicklow tinkers and Mayo would-be murderers, and jolting them into spirited life.

In recent times Hugh Leonard has written about people of his youth and they are now known the world over. John B. Keane has used every snail, saint and sleveen within the shadow of the Stacks for his plays and novels. During a busy Listowel Writers' Week a tinker entered Keane's bar and tried to cadge drinks. Keane ejected him. He returned a few times and the publican took similar action. Next time in, the tinker sat beside me near the door of the premises. 'Do you know why he keeps throwing me out?' he asked. 'You see, he knows that I know that it wasn't himself wrote *Sive* at all, but my father!'

The man was romancing, but in his own way he was close to the mark, for his people indeed presented John B. with his Carthalawn, Pats Bocock and others, just as they offered John's neighbour, Bryan MacMahon, all those raucous characters in his play *The Honey Spike*. A communicator chronicles what he knows.

To direct with precision a stranger entering Delvin from the Mullingar road, no better method could be employed than to have him read Rebecca Kerr's thoughts as she arrived in McDermott's hackney car driven by Paddy McCann. The 'road from the house of God', the 'winding dusty road through Tullahanogue', brings the reader along the way from Delvin to Ballinvalley, just as surely as 'the barrack-like school' and the 'trees surrounding it' tally with the descriptions of former pupils corroborated by photographs. This close identification is open to question. The explicit placing of Garradrimna's premises and residences to coincide with Delvin's suggests intent to ensure recognition.

The Leader of Dublin was one of the first publications to offer a critique on *The Valley of the Squinting Windows*. Its review of 11 May 1918 began:

> It is, in sober truth, a downright shocking book; and as a picture of an 'Irish valley somewhere in the midlands', or anywhere else, it is most assuredly and most grotesquely false to average Irish life. The book is, moreover, the very pith and marrow of cynicism, unrelieved and uncalled-for, captious, sullen, vicious, currish; and the meanly sordid is writ upon its every page.

Against this, A.E. Malone wrote: 'No one can tread on a corn that is not there, but when a scream follows upon the tread it is safe to assume the existence of the corn.'[17]

The Valley of the Squinting Windows had a malign effect on its author's literary career. The sensationalism of its reception obscured MacNamara's subsequent, better work, more deserving of fame than the 'twisted uncharity and calumny of Garradrimna.'[18]

Some Delvin people hold that the event spread a pall over the village that is still sensed. Others allege deficient literacy among some whose education was blighted by the boycott. None can deny the apprehension perceptible whenever the book is discussed. The novel and its aftermath remain suspect topics for conversation, and opinion is given guardedly, or withheld. But at least the windows may now be opened for the people who have inherited that legacy of hurt.

> The one thing that no man can afford, and that nobody but a fool insists on carrying, is a grievance.
>
> George Bernard Shaw
> (letter to Lord Alfred Douglas, 29 May 1931)

EPILOGUE

Would it not be a good idea to ask some society to arrange for a talk on Brinsley's work, with a glance at the ashes of that bonfire in Delvin? The opposition, or should I say the persecution forces, will have withered by now, and somebody could put their case with tenderness. Then there are the survivors of the enlightened and courageous minority who took the author's side, at considerable risk to themselves. Add to that a few writers.[1]

Peadar O'Donnell's suggestion appeared in the first paperback edition of *The Valley of the Squinting Windows* (Dublin 1964), but, to date, has not been acted upon. If the talk ever comes to pass, its location ought to be Delvin, Co. Westmeath.

The school boycott was not solely an Irish phenomenon. At Burston in England a school strike lasted from 1914 until near the start of the Second World War. Teachers Tom and Kathy Higdon came to the Norfolk village determined to improve conditions for their pupils, who were mostly children of farm labourers. They fell foul of their rector and the chairman of the school managers' board – who was a publican and butcher! There were examples of petty tyranny, although not on the Delvin scale, and children were transported to other schools. Like James Weldon, Tom Higdon dabbled in local politics, but the cause of the strike differed from Delvin's and the Burston parents were on the side of their teachers, organizing the boycott as a show of support.

For a different reason Bessie Churchill (from Kilbeggan, in south Westmeath) and Mary O'Sullivan were driven out of Kilclonfert National School in King's County (Offaly) in 1920. On the night of 23 June, armed and masked men entered their residence, 'covered them with revolvers and made a thorough search of the house ... [The leader of the gang] said his orders were that they were to clear out of the district within a month on account of being policemen's wives.'[2] The Board of Education offered little sympathy because their RIC husbands were adequately paid. The women were forced to take refuge in Tullamore barracks.

The *Irish Law Digest* (Dublin 1940) lists a case of conspiracy when a school assistant took on a manager 'for damages to injure her and deprive her of her position in the school.' Other long arguments and strikes have taken place, notably in Sligo (1898), Fanore (1914), Ballymote (1920), Killean (1938) and Ballina (1956-62). Even today a boycott which began in 1986 continues in Recess National School, Connemara. There, Bríd Ní Dhomhnaill sits daily in an empty schoolroom although the situation which brought about the dispute was resolved officially in 1987. Because a book with an imaginative title was at the centre of Delvin's controversy, and because that book was the first of its kind in Ireland, its notoriety spread and endured. When a young girl died in childbirth beside a Marian grotto in Granard, Co. Longford, in February 1984, the town's commissioners demanded an apology from Women's Affairs Minister Nuala Fennell for her reported comment that the affair 'brought back the era of the squinting windows'.[3] Granard in 1984 had no wish to be linked with a Delvin derided in 1918!

The slaughter of sacred cows by Irish writers over a century has pleased some, repelled others. As intimacy with their material grew, authors recognized a duty to set down what they observed. Whether Brinsley MacNamara found his duty a pleasant one or not, he, more than most, carried it out.

> Wasn't it the strangest thing now how she had managed more or less to live it down? But people would remember it all again in the light of this thing ...[4]

And remembering, let them smile this time and breathe a prayer for James Weldon and John, Joseph Clyne and Mary Cully and all the others who walked the 'Road of the Dead' from Delvin.

APPENDIX 1

THE STORY

Mrs Brennan, dressmaker, has an obsessive ambition to see her son, John, ordained a priest, but her path to this glory is shadowed by a past of which she is reminded constantly by the gossiping terror of the valley, Marse Prendergast.

In her youth, Nan Brennan (*née* Byrne) failed to win the heart of wealthy farmer Henry Shannon, and was forced to leave the parish in disgrace having given birth to his child. She had always feared that the infant was murdered and buried in her garden.

She married in England, but foolishly returned to Garradrimna where her husband, Ned, learns of her past from Larry Cully, loafer, and takes to beating her and drinking heavily. Ned's drinking and John's education are financed by Nan's long hours of drudgery at her sewing-machine. She grows increasingly bitter towards Myles Shannon, Henry's brother, to whom she transferred her hatred of the Shannon family after Henry's death. Conniving with the local postmistress, she sends a disparaging letter to his lady friend in England, and the postmistress intercepts the ensuing correspondence. Myles discovers something of this and, in revenge, invites down to Garradrimna his man-about-town nephew Ulick (Henry's son), whom he encourages to lead John Brennan astray. They become good friends, drinking together and generally annoying Nan Brennan.

A pretty young schoolteacher, Rebecca Kerr, attracts the attention of both Ulick and John Brennan, but being a seminarian the latter is reticent about expressing his tender feelings. When Rebecca becomes pregnant by Ulick, a furious John kills his former friend, applies weights to the corpse and submerges it in a lake.

Then, to his horror, John Brennan discovers that his victim was his own half-brother – Nan Byrne's illegitimate child, substituted for the issue from Henry Shannon's brief marriage to Grace Gogarty that had died at birth.

A disgraced Rebecca leaves the valley, and at the end of the novel John Brennan, as drunk as his father ever was, falls through the door and is caught in his demented mother's arms:

> 'O Jesus!' she said.
> There were two of them now.

APPENDIX 2

DRAMATIS PERSONAE

James Weldon	National schoolteacher, father of –
John Weldon	Pseudonym: Brinsley MacNamara
Frances Weldon	Wife of James
Fr Tuite	Parish priest of Delvin 1892-1924
Fr Cogan	Curate at Delvin 1918-22

Allegedly represented in *The Valley of the Squinting Windows* :

Joseph Clyne	Butcher and publican, Delvin
Rose Anne Barry	Schoolteacher, Ballinvalley
Mary Cully	Postmistress, Delvin
Anne Roper	Dressmaker
Richard Roper	Her son
Lord Greville	Wealthy landowner
James Mullen	Local character
Ned Smith	Publican
James Ennis	Amateur actor and entertainer
Ned Leonard	Farmer
Pat Hegarty	Wealthy farmer
	and others.

APPENDIX 3

CHRONOLOGY

1890   John Weldon born 6 September.

1909   John Weldon leaves Delvin to study at Skerries College, Dublin.

1910   Joins Abbey Theatre. Adopts pseudonym, Brinsley MacNamara.

1911   Brinsley MacNamara tours USA with Abbey Theatre Company. James Weldon reported to Board of Education by forged letter.

1913   Brinsley MacNamara returns to Delvin.

1916   *The Valley of the Squinting Windows* written.

1918   *The Valley of the Squinting Windows* published and publicly burned in Delvin. Boycott of James Weldon's school begins.

1919   *The Rebellion in Ballycullen* produced at Abbey Theatre.

1920   *The Irishman, In Clay and in Bronze* and *The Clanking of Chains* published. Brinsley MacNamara marries Helena Degidon in Quin, Co. Clare. *The Land for the People* produced at Abbey Theatre.

1921   *The Mirror in the Dusk* published. Brinsley seriously ill with rheumatic fever in Quin. A son, Oliver, born to Brinsley and Lena.

1923   *The Glorious Uncertainty* produced at Abbey Theatre. James Weldon's case against Fr Tuite and others heard in Dublin. The jury fails to agree.

1925   Brinsley MacNamara appointed temporary Registrar of National Gallery.

1926   Gallery appointment made permanent. *Look at the Heffernans!* produced at Abbey Theatre. James Weldon retires and leaves Delvin. The boycott ends.

1928   *The Master* produced at Abbey Theatre.

1929   *The Various Lives of Marcus Igoe* and *The Smiling Faces* published.

1930   *Return to Ebontheever* published.

1932   Elected member of Irish Academy of Letters.

1933   *Margaret Gillan* produced at Abbey Theatre. James Weldon dies.

1934   *Margaret Gillan* published.

1935   Becomes a Director of the Abbey Theatre. *The Silver Tassie* controversy.

1936   *The Grand House in the City* produced at Abbey Theatre.

1939   Frances Weldon dies. Brinsley MacNamara becomes drama critic of *The Irish Times*.

1941   *The Three Thimbles* produced at Abbey Theatre.

1942   *Return to Ebontheever* reissued as *Othello's Daughter*.

1944   *Look at the Heffernans!* and *The Glorious Uncertainty* translated into Irish.

1945   *Marks and Mabel* produced at Abbey Theatre and published. *Some Curious People* published. Leaves *The Irish Times*.

1946   *Michael Caravan* published.

1949   *Abbey Plays 1899-1948* published.

1951   *The Whole Story of the X.Y.Z.* published.

1960   Resigns from the National Gallery.

1963   Brinsley MacNamara dies 4 February.

1990   *The Burning of Brinsley MacNamara* published 29 November.

APPENDIX 4

THE WRITINGS

Brinsley MacNamara's books, plays, poems, etc.

Books (novels, except where stated)

The Valley of the Squinting Windows (Dublin 1918, London 1918, New York 1919; pbk ed. Dublin 1964, 1968, 1971, 1973, 1976, 1979, 1984, 1989).

The Clanking of Chains (Dublin 1920; pbk ed. 1965, 1984).

In Clay and in Bronze (New York 1920). *The Irishman* (pseud. Oliver Blyth) (London 1920). One and the same.

The Mirror in the Dusk (Dublin 1921).

The Various Lives of Marcus Igoe (London 1929).

The Smiling Faces (short stories) (London 1929).

Return to Ebontheever (London 1930; Dublin 1942 as *Othello's Daughter*).

Some Curious People (short stories) (Dublin 1945).

Michael Caravan (Dublin 1946).

Abbey Plays 1899-1948 (non-fiction) (Dublin 1949).

The Whole Story of the X.Y.Z. (novella) (Belfast 1951).

Plays ([P] signifies subsequent publication)

The Rebellion in Ballycullen, 1919.

The Land for the People, 1920.

The Glorious Uncertainty (P), 1923. Trans. *An Tnúth Cráidhte* (P), 1944.

Look at the Heffernans! (P), 1926. Trans. *Dearc ar na hIfearnánaigh!* (P), 1944.

The Master, 1928.

Margaret Gillan (P), 1933. Trans. *Mairéad Gillan* (P), 1953.

The Grand House in the City, 1936.

The Three Thimbles, 1941.

Marks and Mabel (P), 1945.

The Uncrowned King (co-author with J.H. Perrin).

Published Poetry

'On Seeing Swift in Laracor', *The Oxford Book of Irish Verse* (eds McDonagh & Robinson) (1958).

Irish Weekly Independent: 'The Haunted House' (as Thomas Weldon); 'My Love's Eyes'; 'The Angelus in Summer'; To One Returned'; 'On Reading the Casualty Lists'; 'The Dark Night'; 'October Fields'; 'Any Soldier to Any Sweetheart' (1915). 'Stonebreakers'; 'The Silver Apples of the Moon'; 'From the August Fair'; 'My Loves' (1916). 'The Ploughman of the Sky'; 'Dusk'; 'The High King's Grave'; 'For Helen'; 'The Album Leaves' (1917).

Sunday Independent: 'The Silent Change' (as John Weldon) (1911). 'Old Connor' (1912). 'The Lillies' (1913). 'My Fields of Gold'; 'In Bronze'; 'Summer Pools'; 'The Gate of Doom'; 'The Fairy Army' (1916). 'Portrait of a Girl'; 'O Beauty Calling'; 'Distant Music' (1917).

The Irish Review: 'The Crude Rhyme of the Tinker's Wife' (1912).

The Shamrock: 'The Eternal Hound' (1919).

Published Short Stories

Irish Weekly Independent: 'Mary Galway'; 'Two Letters in a Submarine'; 'The Desert'; 'The Homecoming'; 'Immortal Longings'; 'The Wolves' (1915). 'The End of Hate' (1916). 'The Poet in Exile'; 'The Poet and the Landlady' (Christmas number) (1917). 'The Face of Wonder'; 'The Lover of Fiction' (1918). 'The Return of David Fagan' (Christmas number) (1919). 'The Beard of Stephen Seery' (Christmas number) (1920). 'The Three Mr Darlings' (St Patrick's Day issue) (1921).

Sunday Independent: 'The Poems of Seamus Lavelle'; 'Mirandolina' (1919). 'The Sisters' (1920). 'The Marquis of Clunnen' (1921).

Irish Independent: 'As She Leaves' (1912). 'The Country Dance' (1914).

New Ireland: 'The Shining Horses' (1915). 'Gentlemen – the Police!'; 'An Evening in a Village' (1916).

Evening Telegraph: 'The Sad Philosopher' (1913).

The Freeman's Journal: 'The Going Away' (1913).

The Weekly Freeman's Journal: 'One Woman Only'; 'The Room in Belmore Street' (1919). 'Lovely Mary'; 'The House in Keel'; 'Lovers of the Fields' (1920). 'The Memory of Parnell' (1921).

Living Age: 'The Speechmaker' (1918).

The Shamrock: 'A Patriot' (1919).

The Irish Statesman: 'Patriotism'; 'Dr Oswald Brannigan'; 'The Men Returned'; 'Legislative Men'; 'The Old, Old Men'; 'Men with a Stake in the Country'; 'Political Men'; 'Government Men'; 'The Very Young Men' (1919). 'Comical Men'; 'New Gentlemen'; 'Lonely Men' (1920).

Banba: 'The Picture Gallery'; 'The Comedian' (1921).

The Irish Times: 'The Swan' (1942) (also in *Irishwoman's Journal*, 1968).

Green and Gold: 'The Impossible' (1921). 'Queer Men' (1922).

The Dublin Magazine: 'The Smiling Faces' (1930). 'The Different Mr Darlings' (1931). 'The Hotel' (1942).

The Bell: 'The Master's Holiday' (1947). 'Mullally's Reverie' (1954).

Irish Writing: 'The World and Garrett Reilly' (1950).

'The Cuckoo Clock', *The Penguin New Writing* (ed. John Lehmann) (1942).

Also:

A biographical sketch (22 pp.) entitled 'Growing Up in the Midlands', published posthumously in *The Capuchin Annual* (1964).

A series of twenty-three features on 'Books and Their Writers' for *The Gael* (1921-2).

Articles, criticism, studies, anthologies, radio plays and features, letters to editors. The University of Texas, Austin, Texas, holds a comprehensive collection of manuscripts, drafts and assorted typescripts. The National Library of Ireland holds letters, the original draft of *The Master* (then entitled 'The Boycott', ms. 2107) and of 'The Marquis of Raharney' (ms. 11,939), a comedy in three acts. Also MacNamara's short story 'The Marquis of Clunnen' (ms. 13158-13175).

SOURCES

General

Personal interviews, taped interviews, correspondence outlined in
chapter notes, contemporary newspapers, magazines, etc. Brinsley
MacNamara's writings outlined above. Board of Education files,
National Archives files, State Paper Office files, Public Records files,
NLI mss, Abbey Theatre programmes and minute books. Brinsley
MacNamara's papers, Ballinvalley School registers, Delvin and other
parish records, parish baptismal certificates. 'The Westmeath Outrages'
(paper, 1982), 'Short History of Delvin' (paper, undated), Radio
Éireann transcripts.

Journals etc.

Éire-Ireland, A Journal of Irish Studies, Spring 1968 & Summer 1983.
The Capuchin Annual, 1964.
The Irish Law Digest, 1923.
The Irish Law Directory, 1922-4.
Thom's Irish Who's Who, 1923.
Thom's Directories.

Books

Aldington, Richard, *Lawrence of Arabia* (London 1955).
Anderson, Chester B., *James Joyce* (London 1967).
Ball, F. Elrington, *Judges in Ireland – 1921-1922*, vol. 2 (London 1926).
Bertram, Edward, *The Burston School Strike* (London 1974).
Boylan, Henry, *A Dictionary of Irish Biography* (Dublin 1978).
Boylan, Patricia, *All Cultivated People* (Gerrards Cross 1988).
Brady, Anne M. & Cleeve, Brian, *A Biographical Dictionary of Irish
    Writers* (Gigginstown 1985).

Brady, John, *Short History of the Parishes of the Diocese of Meath* (Navan 1937).

Cogan, A., *The Diocese of Meath – Ancient and Modern*, vol. 3 (Dublin 1870).

Davitt, Michael, *The Fall of Feudalism in Ireland* (London & NY 1904).

Deane, Seamus, *A Short History of Irish Literature* (London 1986).

Fallis, Richard, *The Irish Renaissance* (Dublin 1978).

Fitz-Simon, Christopher, *The Irish Theatre* (London 1983).

Fitzsimons, Hannah, *The Great Delvin* (Delvin 1975).

Healy, John, *History of the Diocese of Meath* (Dublin 1908).

Hobsbaum, Philip, *Essentials of Literary Criticism* (London 1983).

Hogan, Robert, *After the Irish Renaissance* (London 1968).

—— (ed.), *Dictionary of Irish Literature* (Dublin 1980).

—— , *Towards a National Theatre* (Dublin 1970).

Holloway, Joseph, *Joseph Holloway's Abbey Theatre* (Selection) (Illinois 1967).

Hone, Joseph, *W.B. Yeats, 1865-1939* (London 1942).

Hunt, Hugh, *The Abbey* (Dublin 1979).

Keaney, Marian, *Westmeath Authors* (Mullingar 1969).

Kiely, Benedict, *A Letter to Peachtree* (London 1988).

—— , *Modern Irish Fiction* (Dublin 1950).

Lyons, F. S. L., *Ireland Since the Famine* (London 1971).

Macardle, Dorothy, *The Irish Republic* (Dublin 1951).

MacDonagh, Donagh (ed.), *Poems from Ireland* (Dublin 1944).

McHugh, Roger & Harmon, Maurice, *Short History of Anglo-Irish Literature* (Dublin 1982).

Mack, John E., *A Prince of Our Disorder* (London 1976).

MacLysaght, Edward, *Changing Times* (Gerrards Cross 1978).

Moody, T.W. & Martin, F.X., *The Course of Irish History* (Cork 1984).

Murphy, D. J. (ed.), *Lady Gregory's Journals,* Books 1-29 (Gerrards Cross 1978).

O'Connell, T. J., *100 Years of Progress – A History of the I.N.T.O. 1868-1968* (Dublin 1968).

O'Donovan, John, *Ordnance Survey Letters* (Westmeath 1837).

Ó hAodha, Micheál, *Theatre in Ireland* (Oxford 1974).

—— , *The O'Casey Enigma* (Dublin & Cork 1980).

Oram, Hugh, *The Newspaper Book* (Dublin 1983).

Robinson, Lennox, *The Irish Theatre* (London 1939).

Simpson, Alan, *Beckett, Behan and a Theatre in Dublin* (London 1962).

Wade, Allan (ed.), *The Letters of W.B. Yeats* (London 1954).

Walsh, Paul, *Ancient Westmeath* (Gigginstown 1985).

—— , *The Placenames of Westmeath* (Dublin 1957).

Weygandt, Cornelius, *Irish Plays and Playwrights* (Connecticut 1913).

Zamoyska, Betka, *The Burston Rebellion* (London 1985).

NOTES AND REFERENCES

PREFACE

1. Benedict Kiely, 'A Midland Memory', Part Three, *The Irish Times* (26 August 1971).

2. Séamus Ó Saothraí, 'Brinsley MacNamara (1890-1963)', *The Irish Booklover*, vol. 2, no.1 (Spring 1972). The O'Donnell quote is from the preface to the 1964 paperback edition of *The Valley of the Squinting Windows*.

PROLOGUE

1. Hannah Fitzsimons, *The Great Delvin* (Delvin 1975). The author wrote: 'There was no suicidal drowning in any Delvin lake. That referred to in the novel is pure invention'(p.155). She errs both in her inaccuracy (there is no suicidal drowning in the novel) and in implying that everything else described in the book was fact.

ONE – THE BOY

1. Delvin Parish Records.

2. Paul Walsh, 'The Town of the Weir', *The Placenames of Westmeath* (Dublin Institute of Advanced Studies 1957).

3. Brinsley MacNamara, 'Growing Up in the Midlands', *The Capuchin Annual* (1964), p. 149.

4. *Ibid.*, p.152.

5. *Ibid.*, p.154.

6. *The Life of Colman, Son of Luachan*, ed. Kuno Meyer (1858-1919) from a manuscript in the library of Rennes (Dublin 1911).

7.   Padraic O'Farrell, *Fore – The Fact and the Fantasy* (Mullingar 1984), pp. 14-21; 'The Seven Wonders of Fore': the monastery in a bog; the mill without a race; the water that flows uphill; the tree that has three branches (or that won't burn); the water that won't boil; the anchorite in a stone; the stone raised by St Fechin's prayers.

8.   Eileen O'Faolain, *Irish Sagas and Folk-Tales* (Dublin 1954), p. 31.

9.   Brinsley MacNamara, *In Clay and in Bronze* (New York 1920), p. 23.

10.   Brinsley MacNamara, 'Growing Up in the Midlands', p. 159.

11.   Dublin & London 1921.

12.   London 1930.

13.   Rev. John Curry, *The Barbavilla Trials and the Crimes Act in Ireland* (Dublin 1886), a treatise on the proceedings.

14.   Brinsley MacNamara, *Return to Ebontheever* (London 1930), p. 86.

15.   Leading figures in the Irish language revival movement.

16.   Hannah Fitzsimons, *The Great Delvin*, and photographs. Also description by Mr Eugene Doherty, who purchased the school building in 1963, restructured it and taught in it under the name 'Saint Lonan's', a private secondary school, from 1964 to 1969. The free transport scheme made it unviable. Mr Doherty now lives in a bungalow built on the site of the school but has thoughtfully preserved its name-plaque in his gateway. It reads: National School 1834.

17.   Edward King of Williamstown, a senior civil servant, cited by a relative who requests anonymity. Dublin, 20 July 1989.

18.   Brinsley MacNamara, 'Growing Up in the Midlands', p. 167.

19.   *Ibid.,* p. 169. There is no reference to such a performance in the comprehensive list of National Theatre productions listed in *The Abbey 1904-1979* by Hugh Hunt (Dublin 1979), or in the National Theatre archives. The new assistant at Ballinvalley was most probably Joe Eaton.

20.   Gatherings of neighbours in country cottages, not the dances so called at a later stage.

21.   Brinsley MacNamara, *The Clanking of Chains* (Dublin 1965), p. 4.

22.   Tendency to model upon British ways.

23.   Letter from Board of Education File No. 21810, NA. Copy BMP.

24.   Brinsley MacNamara, 'Growing Up in the Midlands', p. 170.

TWO – THE MAN

1. Brinsley MacNamara, *In Clay and in Bronze*, p. 67.

2. Rules of Irish National Theatre Society. NLI ms. 13068(1).

3. Lady Augusta Gregory, *Our Irish Theatre: A Chapter of Autobiography* (Dublin 1914), p. 96.

4. Brinsley MacNamara, *op. cit.*, p. 76.

5. Joseph Holloway's unpublished diaries. NLI ms. 1851.

6. *Ibid.* Also note 6, p. 154 and note on p. 282 of published selection (Illinois 1967).

7. Brinsley MacNamara, 'As She Leaves …: An American Sketch', listed in *Westmeath Authors* (Mullingar 1969).

8. Brinsley MacNamara, 'Old Connor', *Sunday Independent* (16 June 1912); 'Crude Rhyme of the Tinker's Wife: a poem', *Irish Review* (16 June 1912). Both listings in *Westmeath Authors* (Mullingar 1969).

9. Brinsley MacNamara, *In Clay and in Bronze,* pp. 179, 186.

10. *Ibid.*, p. 186.

11. *Ibid.*, pp. 209-10.

12. Seamus O'Sullivan, pseud. of James Sullivan Starkey (1879-1958), influential figure in the Irish Literary Revival; friend of Joyce, Griffith, Gogarty, Yeats, and founder of *The Dublin Magazine* in 1923. Copy of letter is included in Brinsley MacNamara's papers.

13. *Ibid.*

14. Interview with Nellie Weldon, sister of Brinsley MacNamara, before her death in August 1988, recorded by Olive Sharkey at Gaulmoylestown, Mullingar.

15. This estrangement is important. The most serious outcome of the book's publication was to be the harassment of James Weldon by the people of Delvin, who would accuse him of having passed on certain little-known events described in his son's novel (see chapter 5). The father-son relationship at the time makes this seem unlikely. Most commentators agree that Brinsley's source was Séimí Growney. An incident arising out of their friendship may have had an indirect influence on *The Valley of the Squinting Windows*. Hannah Fitzsimons writes (*The Great Delvin*, p. 155):

    > Near Brinsley's home in Ballinvalley was a little grove in which was a large flat stone and to this, Brinsley, with his

writing materials and accompanied by Growney, often repaired. The men's frequenting of the wood was resented by a neighbouring woman, illiterate, who was in the habit of gathering her sprigs there. On one occasion, seeing the writer and his companion leave, she entered the grove and saw, on a large flat stone, a stack of written pages. With some vague hope of keeping the men out of the wood, she gathered the papers in her apron, brought them home and, tying a stone on the bundle of the manuscripts, committed it next day to the waters of nearby Booker's lake.

John Brennan knocks out and drowns his rival, Ulick Shannon, after tying weights to his body. It is interesting to speculate on whether the incident prompted Weldon's piece of 'pure fiction'.

16. NLI ms. 21956(IX) – ACC 3556.

17. Benedict Kiely, 'A Midland Memory'.

THREE – THE BURNING

1. Hannah Fitzsimons, *The Great Delvin*.

2. Interview with Olive Sharkey, Gaulmoylestown, Mullingar, 1988.

3. Hannah Fitzsimons, *op. cit.*, p. 154.

4. Brinsley MacNamara, *VOSW*, p. 42 (pages refer to 1984 paperback edition).

5. *Ibid.*, p. 43.

6. *Ibid.*, pp. 182-3.

7. The family headstone erected by Joseph Clyne in Delvin cemetery does not stipulate that the children died at birth. It merely commemorates 'my two children who died infants'.

8. Evidence of Sergeant Hanna, RIC at the subsequent court case.

9. *Westmeath Examiner*, 22 June 1918.

10. Paul Walsh, *The Placenames of Westmeath*. Also correspondence from Most Rev. Dr M. Smith, Bishop of Meath.

11. *Westmeath Examiner*, 15 December 1923.

12. *Ibid.*, 8 December 1923.

13. *Westmeath Independent*, 8 August 1964.

14. Brinsley MacNamara, 'Three Mad Schoolmasters', from *Some Curious People* (Dublin 1945), pp. 156, 158.

15.   *VOSW*, p. 85. Note the name Mullaghowen. The *Westmeath Examiner* was published in Mullingar.

16.   A reference to Lawrence Ginnell's cattle-drives of 1907.

17.   Accurate assessment of the *Irish Times* review of 8 June 1918.

18.   Topical case at the time of interview, this became known as 'The Kerry Babies' case. Nellie was probably attempting to illustrate how pressure can be put on a community to act against its principles.

19.   *Delvin Parish Magazine* (1987).

FOUR – THE BOYCOTT

1.   Brinsley MacNamara, *Michael Caravan* (Dublin 1946), pp. 67, 115-16.

2.   *Westmeath Examiner*, 22 June 1918. It put the number of pupils at three.

3.   The *Irish Times* court case report, 5 December 1923. Cully was Delvin's postmaster at time of book's publication.

4.   Description by Seamus Leonard, Ballinvalley, Delvin.

5.   T. J. O'Connell, *100 Years of Progress – A History of the I.N.T.O. 1868-1968* (Dublin 1968). A revision of the Resolution in June 1916 added that 'the bishops will interpret the said Resolution in the sense suggested by the teachers, namely, that the teacher shall be afforded an opportunity of being heard in his own defence before he is either summarily dismissed or served with notice of dismissal'. The Resolution was embodied as a statute in the National Synod of Maynooth in 1927 (Statute No. 387).

6.   *Westmeath Examiner*, 22 June 1918.

7.   SPO, Ref. 1918 A-K/15129. A further complaint was made on 5 August.

8.   SPO, Crime Branch Special, Carton 23. Order Number 16, affecting Westmeath, was issued on 14 June.

9.   At the subsequent trial (*q.v.*) James Weldon claimed that the document was dictated by Fr Cogan, who told him that if he did not sign it, his son would be arrested. The statement expressed Weldon's sorrow for any offence given by the publication of the book. Fr Cogan also told him, he claimed, that if he signed the children would be sent back to school.

10.   Brinsley MacNamara, *The Various Lives of Marcus Igoe* (London 1929), p. 183.

11.   Prefatory note to Brentano, New York edition, 1919.

12.   Letter from Board of National Education to Fr Tuite. Form of greeting: 'Rev. Sir'. Board of Education File No. 2862.

13.   Prefatory note to Brentano edition. MacNamara quoted incorrectly. The extract as written by Synge goes:

> 'And asking your pardon, is it you's the man killed his father?'
> 'I am, God help me!'
> 'Then my thousand welcomes to you ...'

Among Brinsley MacNamara's papers is a note saying Delvin people 'expected me to do the Playboy on them'. Note the upper-case in 'Press'!
The book was not generally well received. See the *Irish Times* review on p. 79.

14.   Typed on plain paper signed 'Brinsley MacNamara'. File No. 28881, NA. Copy BMP.

15.   Brinsley MacNamara, *In Clay and in Bronze,* pp. 78, 115-16.

16.   Andrew E. Malone, 'Brinsley MacNamara – An Appreciation', *The Dublin Magazine* (July 1929), p. 53.

17.   *The Clanking of Chains,* p. 72.

18.   Benedict Kiely, *Modern Irish Fiction* (Dublin 1950), p. 15.

19.   Abbey Theatre Programme, National Theatre Archives.

20.   Brinsley MacNamara, *The Mirror in the Dusk* (Dublin 1921), p. 63.

21.   Andrew E. Malone, *op. cit.*

22.   Delvin Parish Records contain a survey of parochial property carried out by James Weldon. Correspondence undated.

23.   Letter from Mícheál Ó hAodha to Padraic O'Farrell, Padraic O'Farrell, *The Sean MacEoin Story* (Cork 1981).

24.   Robert Hogan (ed.), *Dictionary of Irish Literature* (London & Basingstoke 1980).

25.   Copy of Fr Cogan's letter from File No. 28881, NA. Copy BMP.

26.   From File No. 28881, NA. Copy BMP.

27.   *Ibid.*

28.   *Ibid.*

29.   *Ibid.*

30.   *VOSW,* p. 42.

31.   Interview with Mrs Rose Doyle, Moyleroe, Delvin, who was born on New Year's Day 1900. Also *Delvin Parish Magazine* (1988).

32. Allan Wade, *The Collected Letters of W.B. Yeats*, vol. 2 (London 1954).

33. BMP. Paraphrasing by Padraic O'Farrell from narration by Oliver Weldon, 20 July 1989.

FIVE – THE TRIAL

1. Brinsley MacNamara, *The Various Lives of Marcus Igoe*, p. 50.

2. Lennox Robinson, *The Irish Theatre*. Lectures delivered during Abbey Theatre Festival, Dublin, August 1938. NLI 82209 R1.

3. Board of Education File No. 2862.

4. Interview with Benedict Kiely, Donnybrook, 15 June 1989.

5. No newspaper reports or official documentation gives the judge's Christian name. Two Lord Chief Justices named O'Connor were in office then. The Master of the Rolls, Charles A. O'Connor, was remembered for making absolute an order for a writ of habeas corpus in respect of IRA prisoners in Cork and Limerick, Egan and Higgins by name. He thus declined to follow the unanimous decision of the King's Bench in identical cases. The ruling was a blow to military rule and the military authorities refused to produce the two men. O'Connor considered this contempt of court and issued a writ of attachment against British C. in C. General Macready, General Strikland, Colonel Cameron and the Governors of Cork and Limerick jails. 'It must have then occurred to him that the continued existence of his court at all was due to the presence of British troops,' said Macready. O'Connor retorted: 'I don't know if it is intended to resist the writ of the court by force of arms. If that is the case we have come to the days of red ruin and the breaking up of the laws.' There were no arrests, however. Refs Sir Nevil Macready, *Annals of an Active Life*, vol. 2 (London 1924); Dorothy Macardle, *The Irish Republic* (Dublin 1951).

   Chief Justice James O'Connor had conversations with prominent people during the Treaty negotiations. These included A. W. Cope, Assistant Under-Secretary for Ireland, Lloyd George and Edward Carson. Legal memories are convinced that Charles A., Master of the Rolls, was the presiding judge.

6. Brinsley MacNamara, 'Three Mad Schoolmasters', p. 176.

7. Joseph Holloway Diaries. NLI ms. 1851.

8. BMP.

9. *Ibid.*

10. Board of Education File No. 2862. An amusing memo from a civil servant adds: 'It is probable that MacNamara will try to see the Minister as he is pretty well known to Mr McNeill.' Eoin McNeill was the scholar, poet, founder-

member of the Gaelic League and former Chairman of the Irish Volunteers (1913) who became first Minister for Education in the Saorstát Éireann government.

11. *Ibid.*

12. Brinsley MacNamara, 'Three Mad Schoolmasters', p. 161.

13. Brinsley MacNamara, *The Various Lives of Marcus Igoe*, p. 12.

SIX – THE BOOK

1. Brinsley MacNamara, *In Clay and in Bronze*, pp. 115-16.

2. Andrew E. Malone, 'Brinsley MacNamara – An Irish Realist', *The Bookman* (June 1928).

3. Radio discussion. Last of a series entitled 'The Writer and the Community'. Benedict Kiely and Eavan Boland, RTE.

4. *Ibid.*

5. Letter to author, 9 July 1989.

6. *Irish Independent*, 7 February 1964.

7. *Ibid.*, 5 February 1963.

8. *Ibid.*, 5 February 1963.

9. Thomas Flanagan, *Irish Press*, 18 July 1964; Sean McMahon, *Éire-Ireland*, vol. 3, no. 1 (Spring 1968).

10. Robert Hogan (ed.), *Dictionary of Irish Literature* (Dublin 1980).

11. *Ibid.*, pp. 418-20.

12. Interview with Benedict Kiely, Donnybrook, 15 June 1989.

13. Richard Fallis, *The Irish Renaissance* (Dublin 1978), p. 205.

14. *Éire-Ireland*, vol. 3, no. 1 (Spring 1968).

15. *Ibid.*, vol. 18, no. 2 (Summer 1983).

16. McHugh & Harmon, *Short History of Anglo-Irish Literature* (Dublin 1982), p. 273.

17. Seamus Deane, *A Short History of Irish Literature* (London 1986), p. 200.

18. *The Irish Times*, 11 August 1984.

19. Brinsley MacNamara, *The Various Lives of Marcus Igoe*, pp. 105-6.

SEVEN – THE SEQUEL

1.   Brinsley MacNamara, *In Clay and in Bronze*, p. 262.

2.   File No. 28881, NA.

3.   Robert Hogan (ed.), *Dictionary of Irish Literature*, p. 419.

4.   Donagh MacDonagh (ed.), *Poems from Ireland* (Dublin 1944), pp. 32-4.

5.   Hugh Hunt, *The Abbey*, p. 133.

6.   *The Irish Times*, 28 August 1935.

7.   *Ibid.*

8.   Interview with Benedict Kiely, Donnybrook, 20 July 1989.

9.   Letter from Mícheál Ó hAodha, 9 July 1989.

10.   *The Irish Times*, 11 August 1984.

11.   Interview with Benedict Kiely, Donnybrook, 20 July 1989. An oral version of a story told in *A Letter to Peachtree* (London 1988), p. 154.

12.   Seamus Kelly, 'Portrait of a Playwright', *RTE Guide*, vol. 3, no. 31 (29 July 1966). The bar was Kennedy's. Brinsley also frequented The Scotch House.

13.   View of a close relative who wishes to remain anonymous.

14.   Brinsley MacNamara, *Michael Caravan*, p. 318.

15.   See note 9 above.

16.   Interview with Seán Mac Réamoinn, Dublin, 20 July 1989.

17.   *VOSW*, p. 223.

EIGHT – THE 'VALLEY'

1.   Brinsley MacNamara, 'Growing Up in the Midlands', p. 149.

2.   Mullingar 1985.

3.   'The Westmeath Outrages 1868-1871', paper by Christopher Murphy O'Connor (January 1982), Westmeath County Library.

4.   Michael Davitt, *The Fall of Feudalism in Ireland* (London & New York 1904), pp. 42-3.

5.   Brinsley MacNamara, *Michael Caravan*, p. 86.

6.   John Healy, *History of the Diocese of Meath*, vol. 3 (Dublin 1908), pp. 86-7.

7.   *Ibid*.

8.   A. Cogan, *The Diocese of Meath – Ancient and Modern*, vol. 3 (Dublin 1870), p. 34.

9.   Brinsley MacNamara, *Some Curious People*, p. 152.

10.   *VOSW*, p. 15.

11.   Anonymous contributor.

12.   *VOSW*, p. 35.

13.   *Ibid.*, p. 103.

14.   *Ibid.*, p. 41.

15.   *Ibid.*, p. 86.

16.   James Joyce, *Ulysses* (Paris 1922). Opening passage.

17.   A. E. Malone, 'Brinsley MacNamara – An Appreciation' (1929).

18.   Benedict Kiely, *Modern Irish Fiction*, p. 41.

EPILOGUE

1.   Peadar O'Donnell, Preface to Anvil paperback edition of *The Valley of the Squinting Windows* (1964).

2.   Other parallels in the Burston School Strike included false letters sent to the Norfolk Education Committee and Tom Higdon's rating being given as 'Excellent' throughout. J. J. Bussens, landlord of The Jolly Farmers, behaved exactly like Joseph Clyne in Delvin. The Kilclonfert case was political, the result of War of Independence activities. See Betka Zamoyska, *The Burston Rebellion* (London 1985); B. Edwards, *The Burston School Strike* (London 1974); TCL Pb-63-876 and P40304. For the Kilclonfert case, see SPO, CSORP 2489/1922. Quotation from Constable Churchill's statement of 16 April 1931 to National Board of Education.

3.   Molloy *v.* Gallagher and Egan, NLI 346/R2.

4.   *Irish Press*, 16 February 1984.

5.   *VOSW*, p. 220.